Published 2011 by Veritas Publications
7–8 Lower Abbey Street
Dublin 1, Ireland
publications@veritas.ie
www.veritas.ie

ISBN 978-1-84730-331-8

10 9 8 7 6 5 4 3 2 1

Image on p. 167 courtesy of John Quinn. Lines from 'All Souls' Night' by Michael Coady (p. 22), from *All Souls* (1997) by kind permission of the author and The Gallery Press, www.gallerypress.com. Lines from 'Ploughman' (p. 46) and 'The Great Hunger' (p. 72) by Patrick Kavanagh are reprinted from *Collected Poems*, edited by Antoinette Quinn (Allen Lane, 2004), by kind permission of the Trustees of the Estate of the late Katherine B. Kavanagh, through the Jonathan Williams Literary Agency. Lines by James Reeves (p. 56), from *The Blackbird in the Lilac* (Oxford University Press, 1962). Lines by Iona and Peter Opie (p. 66), from *I Saw Esau* (Walker Books, 1947). Lines from 'Peeling Potatoes' (p. 74), from *The Haw Lantern*' (Faber and Faber, 1987), and 'Station Island' (p. 152) from *Station Island* (Faber and Faber, 1984), by Seamus Heaney, 'Snapshot' by Robyn Rowland (p. 102), from *Seasons of Doubt and Burning: New and Selected Poems* (Five Islands Press, 2010), by kind permission of the author. Verses from 'A Grand Tour' by Mike Cooley (pp. 124–5), by kind permission of the author. 'Scintillate' (p. 165) from *You at the Back: Collected Poems 1967–1987* (Jonathan Cape, 1991), and 'Survivor' (p. 165), by Roger McGough.

A catalogue record for this book is available from the British Library.

Cover designed by Barbara Croatto, Veritas;
illustrations by Loreto Reilly
Printed in Ireland by Turners Printing Company Ltd, Longford

Veritas books are printed on paper made from the wood pulp of managed forests. For every tree felled, at least one tree is planted, thereby renewing natural resources.

IN MEMORY OF NOEL QUINN (1939–2011)

Contents

Foreword 9

Moments 11

Transience 13

The Pearl of Autumn 14

The Land of Make-Believe 15

Ruby 16

A Text Message 17

The Gift 18

A Summer Christmas 19

The Breastplate 20

The Old House 21

The Names They Had 22

Worms 23

A Leaf from a Distant Land 24

A Letter to the Editor 1 25

Teacher 26

The Wee Hammer 27

Why? 28

Bookmarks 29

Longing for Home 30

An Aural Theatre 31

The Angel in the Green 32

Mad Cow 33

The Ring 34

At Play 35

Dogger 36

A Handy Moment 1 — The Struggle 37

A Handy Moment 2 — The White Stone 38

A Handy Moment 3 — Enough 39

A Letter to the Editor 2 40

In Paradiso 41

Sandra 42

Cloneycavan Man 43

Birth of a Song 44

Uncle Jimmy 46

Easter Dawn 47

Farewell to John 48

Possibility 50

Márla-fied 51

A Walk Into History 52

An Old Photograph 53

Rock of Ages 54

Teaching Debut 55

Cows 1 56

Cows 2 57

A Double Blow 58

Bobby 59

The Voice 60

Pigs 61

The Lure of Letters 1 62

The Lure of Letters 2 63

The Lure of Letters 3 64
Bhutan 65
A Twenty-Cent Treasure 66
Boarding 67
The Library of Friends 68
The Goal 69
Streetwise 70
The Best Medicine 71
Naming the Fields 72
November 73
In the Barrack Garden 74
Leaving Otterbrook 75
Sing! Sing! Sing! 76
Lir 77
Boghomage 1 – The Poet 78
Boghomage 2 – The Artist 79
In Auschwitz 80
Father and Son 81
Funny You Should Say That 82
An Ordinary Wee Draper 83
Keeping Going 84
Another Text Message 85
A Hive of Industry 86
The Dying Year 87
A Sixpenny Treasure 88
Star 89
Stone Walls 90
Forbidden Fruit 91

Finding a Balance 92
Heroes 93
In Highgate Cemetery 94
Seen and Not Heard 96
Entombed 97
Two Ladies 98
Broadcasting Debut 99
A Week of Moments 100
Lazy Days 102
Katie 103
My Education 104
Tacit Knowledge 105
The Beauty of Water 106
Fear 108
Made to Measure 109
Questioning George 110
The Kitchen 111
Bees 112
Infinity 113
Hope 114
A Letter to the Editor 3 115
Peas in Our Time 116
Early Reading 117
Teenager 118
A Bilk Moment 119
Doing Nothing 120
Life 121
Salt and Pepper 122

A Child's Gift 123
Below the Salt 124
The Music of Words 126
A Favourite Prayer 127
Cramming 128
On Being Brave 129
My Gardening Companion 130
Elsewhere 131
Meandering 132
Astrud Gilberto Saves Ireland! 133
The Return 134
Eccentrics 135
The Music Box 136
Nightlight 137
Enthusiasm 138
Bears and Circuses 139
STOP PRESS! 140
Drains and Radiators 141
Regarding Clichés 142
Two Hundred Valentines 143
Rite of Passage 144
Butterflies 145
In Coole Park 146
An Ordinary Ould Sunday 147
Right Pleasure 148
Anniversary Gift 149
Making Contact 150
Beautiful People 151
The Wisdom of Three Poets 152
Daydreaming 153
A Chance Remark 154
Me and Daniel – A Weather Conversation . . . 155
A Quare Quiz 156
In the Presence of Holiness 157
The Miracle of Us 158
Brendan 159
Up the Bridge! 160
The Company of Books 161
The Beauty of Age 162
Writing Simple 163
Precious Stones 164
Roger 165
Out for the Day 166
First Rose of Summer 167
A Portrait of the Artist 168
Benedictus 169
At Rest 170
Excuse me, Ma'am 171
Garret 172
Strangers on a Train 173
Be Quiet! 175
And Finally 176

Thank You for the Moments 177
Epilogue 179

Foreword

THIS ENGROSSING BOOK OF CAPTURED moments is full of wonder, surprise, joy, tenderness, humour, consolation, solace and deep insight.

Pause, open and read any page of this book and you will experience a glorious moment. It takes a minute or less to read any of these 'moments', but concealed within each one, beyond the printed word and story – in their spirit, their mood and their atmosphere – lies a wisdom, an incitement to seize the moment, to find the wonder in the ordinary.

Through these short and powerful meditations, based on his own authentic experiences, John reveals his practice of mindfulness. Joining him on these real-life experiences will open our eyes, our hearts and our minds. What is clear is that, in all our journeying, what matters most is not where we are going, but how we are here – in this present moment.

All our moments are wonderful but they are transitory. The past has gone, the future is yet to come – we have only now. It is how we receive and experience this moment that matters. The real wisdom of this book lies in John's response to each situation, each experience, each event, each moment that matters. The present is a dynamic reality that cannot be boxed or defined. It can only be experienced. John's moments pause life in every direction, catch a snapshot, and invite us simply to look here – wherever we happen to be, however we are feeling – and allow the insight of the moment to transform us.

When we are mindful, when we are aware of what we are doing, we are present and attentive to each moment. These moments all reflect what it is to have a meaningful, nourishing, spiritual life, where everything is viewed in a way that deepens and makes it more significant. John shares himself with us in a compassionate manner that feeds and enlivens our souls.

These are John's reflections on parts of his life as it happens to him and around him. They are unpretentious and do not preach, but I hope they will help us all to stop, to pause, to be – just for a moment – and they will lead us to search for the spiritual and deeper meaning, not in the exotic or unreachable, but right here where we are – in the ordinariness of everyday life.

– SR STANISLAUS KENNEDY

Moments

There are in our existence spots of time
That with distinct pre-eminence retain
A renovating virtue whence ... our minds
Are nourished and invisibly repaired;
A virtue, by which pleasure is enhanced ...
Such moments
Are scattered everywhere, taking their date
From our first childhood.

— WILLIAM WORDSWORTH, THE PRELUDE

MOMENTS SCATTERED EVERYWHERE. IN the words we use, in innocent incidents, chance meetings. In letters and text messages. In natural phenomena. In lines of poetry, anecdotes. In the comings and goings of everyday life.

Moments is a personal collection of words, events, experiences, observations that console, cheer, nourish, heal. Moments that are brief and sometimes fleeting but, once caught and held, offer meaning to our lives and bear significance in their very simplicity. They open the door into what Yeats called 'the rag and bone shop of the heart ...'

— JOHN QUINN

Transience

A FEW YEARS AGO I GAVE A TALK IN ST Kieran's College, Kilkenny. As I entered the college grounds, I noticed an inscription carved in stone above the gate – *Hiems transiit*. Having been a decent Latin scholar in my day, I could translate this straight away as 'Winter has passed', but I was puzzled as to its significance. I subsequently discovered it was the school's motto. St Kieran's was founded in 1782 after the passing of the Relief Act of that year which enabled Catholics to set up schools. 'Winter' was a metaphor for the Penal Laws which had deprived them of such liberties for the best part of a century. It had truly been a long winter, but it had passed.

As all things do, if only we have patience. We rail against the harshness of our own winters, whether it be severe weather conditions or the current economic winter – but they will pass. John O'Donohue liked to tell of a contest that was held in ancient Greece to find a sentence that would somehow always be true. The winning sentence was 'This too will pass'. He further quoted St Teresa of Avila, who said that no matter how difficult and lonesome times may be, we should be consoled by the knowledge that these too will pass. So be it a week of ice and snow, an economic recession or a century's penal times – winter will always pass. It is carved in stone.

The Pearl of Autumn

MID-SEPTEMBER. WARM, SETTLED WEATHER has given way to blustery gales. The first chestnuts have crashed to earth, shattering their spiky shells and dislodging the nuts within from their creamy casings. I pick one up on my way home from the shops and caress it between my fingers.

It is a thing of rare beauty in its smoothness and its sheen. An annual autumn miracle. I marvel at the contours of its grain and the gloss of its distinctive colour. It heralds the onset of autumn and the loss of long summer evenings, but for now its sheer beauty captivates me.

I place the chestnut in a wooden bowl on the hall table. Soon it will wizen and wither, but for now on this September afternoon, untimely ripped from its protective shell, it is truly a delight to feel and fondle and simply behold. It is the pearl of autumn.

The Land of Make-Believe

THERE IS A HAPPY LAND, BELOVED OF children, where they find respite, comfort and privacy. It is the land of make-believe. It is a land much sought by only children, as Peter Ustinov told me in an interview on his childhood.

'I loved cars, while my parents couldn't drive and knew or cared nothing about cars. It is hard to explain how humiliating that was in an urban society. At the Sports Day in my preparatory school, there was even a chauffeurs' race. Not having a car, we didn't have a chauffeur of course, but I had a very rich friend, a boy whose family had two chauffeurs and he offered me the slower of the two for the race. That was beyond my capacity for endurance so I declined and as a consequence of that humiliation I became a car …

'I was a car and I worried my parents considerably. I switched myself on in the morning. I didn't say very much. I drove around all day and then backed myself into bed at night and switched off. I was an Amilcar, a French car of fragile appearance, making an enormous amount of noise. It wasn't very fast but it pleased me enormously. Probably because I felt a nascent corpulence, I was devoted to that small, svelte, slim French car. I remember how it sounded when it had a flat battery on those days when I didn't feel too well *(he mimics the sound of an engine slowly turning over and 'dying').*

'Once when we visited my maternal grandfather in Estonia, I was busy being a car while my mother was suffering from a toothache – I could hear the moans from under her yellow cloche hat. I was in particularly frisky form – a lot of gear changes and sharp gradients – so she shouted loudly at me. Her father intervened – "Don't do that! Don't think of it as a motor-car but as the sound of his imagination developing, and you will find it tolerable."'

Ruby

A RECENT TELEVISION DOCUMENTARY SENT me searching in my memory box. There it was among the match programmes, letters and assorted photographs – the autograph book. A prized possession of my teenage years – covered in the style of textbooks of the period, in strong brown paper.

My autograph period in my mid-teens coincided with the great days of Santry Stadium when Billy Morton brought the world's top athletes to Dublin. And here they are – the great Herb Elliott, Peter Snell, Merv Lincoln, Gordon Pirie, as well as our own Ronnie Delaney and Eamonn Kinsella. Memories of that wonderful night when the first five home in the mile event were under four minutes. Here too is Italian cycling legend, Fausto Coppi.

My other great sporting passion of those years was tennis. Again the autograph book brims with legends of the sport – Lew Hoad, Tony Trabert, Jaroslav Drobny, Ashley Cooper. (Quite a collection – wonder should I put it on eBay!) But sporting heroes are not my concern just now. Somewhere in this little book is another treasure.

A memory of a murky winter evening in Dublin. I am loitering outside the stage door of the Theatre Royal, pen and autograph book at the ready. The door opens. She steps out, a petite figure, swathed in a full-length fur coat, her eyes sparkling in a dazzling smile. I nervously mumble my request. 'Of course,' comes the husky reply. As she writes, I stumble through telling her how wonderful her show was. 'Oh, you're very kind,' she purrs and hands me the book as she enters the waiting taxi. *Love, Ruby Murray* is the beautifully written message. I dream my way home on the number 15 bus.

A Text Message

SOMETIMES THE SEEMINGLY MOST TRIVIAL event can blow your heart wide open.

I am sitting at home on a lazy Sunday afternoon wading through the newspapers, when the gentle *parrup* on my mobile phone tells me I have 'one message received'. I open it. It has come from our daughter Deirdre in distant Long Island.

I'm home cleaning, listening to Ray Charles and roasting a chicken. The sounds and the smells remind me of home and you and mum …

There are only two things I want to say:

1. Some thirty years previously, an ordinary old lazy Sunday had created a memory for a young girl. Father pottering about. Mother listening to Ray Charles. Chicken roasting in the oven. Children at play. An ordinary old Sunday. A nothing day. But the comfort of the sounds and the smells were seeping into a child's subconscious and would lie there until reawakened in her own little cottage three decades later and three thousand miles distant.

2. It is probably the most beautiful text message I will ever receive.

The Gift

Lifelines WAS A SERIES OF THREE BOOKS IN which 'famous' people chose and wrote about their favourite poems. The idea was the brainchild of students from Wesley College, Dublin, and the royalties from all three best-selling collections went toward funding projects in the developing world.

When I was asked to nominate a poem, my initial reaction was to choose a piece by Kavanagh, but then I remembered a little poem I had come across twenty years earlier. I was editing an anthology for primary schools and was anxious to include some children's writing. A teacher from Duleek, Co. Meath, had sent me a poem – 'Things I Like' – by a pupil of his, Patricia Heeney, aged twelve. For me the poem had a simplicity, a directness and a freshness that time had not withered (and still has not withered, another twenty years on). There is the reassurance of the familiar, allied to a natural poetic rhythm.

Truly, Patricia had the gift. I hope she is still writing!

THINGS I LIKE
Bark of our dog to welcome us home,
Croak of a frog on the commons;
Trot of a horse,
Heather and gorse on Bellewstown Hill;
Bleat of a lamb,
Gurgling and laughing of Curleys' baby
In her pram.

I really love that poem!

A Summer Christmas

IT HAD BEEN A HORRIFIC TIME. IN DECEMBER she had fallen down stone stairs and broken her neck. Three months in hospital, her head encaged in that awful metal halo. No sooner out of hospital than her sister dies suddenly. A long road to recovery. To make up for the Christmas spent in hospital I would bring her for a week to Kelly's Hotel in Rosslare.

June 25th, 2001. A Summer Christmas. Our first day in Kelly's. A warm, humid day. Sound of the surf as we relax in the hotel garden. Contentment. An enjoyable lunch together. Back to the garden. Relaxed. No need for conversation. Good to be here. Christmas Day. Champagne for dinner tonight.

Late afternoon. She decides to go for a swim in the sea. I take her hand and guide her down the steep sand dune. Watch from the dune as she enters the water. She splashes down and begins swimming. One, two, three strokes. So proud of her, after all the trauma she has been through. I expect her to wave in triumph. Then nothing. Head stays down in the water. Trouble. Jesus, no, please. I race into the water and drag her out. Please, please, please. No. No. No. Others arrive. A doctor, a lifeguard. They try to resuscitate her, but it is hopeless. I look at the limp body, the beautiful hair bedraggled and matted with sand. She is gone. Gone. Gone. Gone. Others comfort me, but I am numb.

I have known her for thirty-five years, been married to her for thirty-three. Now the ultimate moment of horror is here. My wife and the only love of my life, Olive McKeever, lies dead on Rosslare beach on Christmas Day in Summer.

The Breastplate

WE LEARNED AT SCHOOL HOW ST PATRICK raised the ire of King Laoire when he lit the paschal fire on the Hill of Slane. The king summoned Patrick to Tara next day to explain his actions. But the druids, who were even more fearful than the king, set out to ambush and kill Patrick and his followers as they made their way to the royal palace.

As they waited, they heard chanting from the approaching group. Soon they could discern the words …

Christ before me
Christ behind me
Christ on my right hand
Christ on my left

This was *Lúireach Phádraig* – St Patrick's Breastplate – a shield that no human weapon could pierce. The assailants were mystified, even more so when all they could see passing by was a flock of deer. The miraculous disguise and the lengthy chant ensured that Patrick and his company reached Tara safely. A fanciful tale, but a rather wonderful one! The chant or hymn became known as 'The Deer's Cry'.

Over fifteen centuries later, in a Midlands boarding school, I would recite that hymn together with my fellow-students at the end of our night prayers in the school oratory …

Christ in every eye that sees me
Christ in every ear that hears me

For we were under the care of the Patrician Brothers. It was our Breastplate too.

The Old House

OLD DERELICT HOUSES FASCINATE ME. THEY arouse my curiosity. Who lived there? For how long? What was their story? Their joys and their sorrows? Why did they leave? Every house has a story to tell.

I passed one house recently that particularly intrigued me. The house itself was intact but all the windows and doors had been bricked up. A huge tangle of briars and nettles advanced up its walls. I stopped at the entrance – a rusted broken gate. Here was a story, surely. Trapped within this concrete tomb must be memories wafting through the shell from room to room.

The joy that might have filled a young couple when they crossed its new-laid threshold. The songs that might have echoed through its rooms. The laughter of children, maybe. The cries of pain. Sorrow, hurt, disappointment. Days of happiness and nights of delight. Lives lived. Death encountered. Mystery. Abandonment.

I am startled by a strange noise. A keening echo from within the tomb? I step back uneasily. Maybe I have disturbed long-quiet spirits – or maybe it is a cry from the past. I listen again. It is the wind sighing through the broken metal tubing of the gate. I chide myself for being so fanciful. I retreat to my car. Still …

The Names They Had

IT STRIKES ME THAT NICKNAMES ARE NOT as popular today as in times past. A nickname could be a malicious infliction but for the most part it was applied with affection, often to pay tribute to physical prowess (Stonewall Dixon), to identify a particular habit (a drover from my native village was named 'Rooster' for his habit of sleeping in a tree to be near the cattle in his care), or simply to acknowledge his profession (my father the sergeant was known as 'The Skipper').

In his marvellous poem 'All Souls', Michael Coady meets some of the characters who inhabited his native Carrick-on-Suir, as he makes his way home from the pub on All Souls' Night …

… including Cromwell and William of Orange
Daniel O'Connell and Mary Spake Aisy
Cough No More and Boil 'Em In Oil
Féach Amach and Pingin Fé Chloch
Peggy's Leg and Pull Through

The Sleepy Tailor and All is Well
Red Spinner and Rattle the Latch
Seán a Mham and Fear Bocht
Blue Lookout and Hole in the Wall
Hat o'Thrushes and Hot Fomentation
Pigeon's Milk and Khyber Pass
Laredo and Moscow and Oilcan and Oxo
Bengal Lancer and Mary Game Ball --
On this grounded night I meet them all.

What a story each of *them* would have to tell!

Worms

I TUMBLE THE MASS OF DAMP SOIL OUT OF the plastic bag and onto the newspapers that I have laid across the teacher's desk. There is an initial silence from the children, then a few nervous giggles as life squirms its way through and out of the soil. Worms. Ten excellent specimens from my own garden.

'Now, I want you to take a worm, carefully and gently, in your hands and observe it closely – its movement, its structure, its colours. Feel it. Talk to it. Then write about the experience …' There are a few shrieks of 'No way!' Some children just will not touch the wriggly creatures, but most of them accede to my wishes.

I have been prompted to try this experiment by two people. One is Mike Cooley, engineer and writer, who had bemoaned the fact that children today have such little primary knowledge of the natural world. 'They know so much about so many creatures but it's all secondary knowledge, derived from the internet, television etc. How many of them have actually experienced a worm wriggling in their hands?' The other is Richard Louv, who makes the same point in his book, *Last Child in the Woods: Saving Our Children from Nature Deficit Disorder*. For Louv, children are missing the tactile sensory experience that is central to their development and mental health. For today's children, 'nature is more abstraction than reality … a recent television ad depicts a four-wheel-drive SUV racing along a breathtakingly beautiful mountain stream while in the back seat two children watch a movie on a flip-down video screen.'

The children wash their hands and write sensitively about their unusual experience. I return the worms and their habitat to the plastic bag. No worm was harmed in this experiment. Later, I will return them to my vegetable patch where no doubt they will wreak revenge on my potatoes.

A Leaf from a Distant Land

I HOLD IN MY HAND A LEAF THAT HAS BEEN pressed dry between the pages of a book. The leaf has come from a far distant woodland, and to touch it brings back a memory of a wonderful day. The book in which it rests gives a clue. Its title is *Lev Tolstoy and Yasnaya Polyana*. On the flyleaf I have written – *Purchased at Yasnaya Polyana, Thursday, Sept. 25th 2003, for 500 rubles.*

Yasnaya Polyana is a largely wooded estate about two hundred kilometres from Moscow, and it was here that Leo Tolstoy was born and spent most of his life. It was here that the great novels *War and Peace* and *Anna Karenina* were realised. And it was here on a September afternoon in 2003 that I came to pay homage to this great writer with a group of Irish tourists.

We walked the long avenue flanked by majestic silver birches until it emerged before us – a large rambling two-storey white house. A woman greets us. In bearing and dress she might well have stepped out of a Tolstoy novel. She guides us through the house – kitchen, dining room, living rooms, bedrooms – all as they would have been in Tolstoy's day. Most fascinating is his study – the Persian walnut desk with books strewn where he had left them, candles where he had snuffed them. What extraordinary journeys of the imagination had taken place in this room! There is a wonderful sense of presence here – as if the great man had just stepped outside …

The woodlands are truly beautiful. No wonder Tolstoy loved this place. Our guide leads us through leafy walkways, past the 'love-tree' – two trees that have entwined each other – until we reach Tolstoy's resting-place, a simple unmarked grassy mound, deep in the woods. A sacred silence pervades.

I replace the leaf opposite a Tolstoy quotation:

Without my Yasnaya Polyana I would have a hard time imagining Russia and my relation to her …

A Letter to the Editor 1

Stradbally North
Clarinbridge

8 Sept 2005

The Editor
The Irish Times
Dublin 2

Dear Madam,

While driving from Limerick to Dublin this week, approaching Roscrea, a large National Roads Authority sign caught my eye. Regarding local roadworks, the sign proudly proclaims that this is the:

N7 – INANE REALIGNMENT

When I eventually regained control of my steering, I thought – fair play to the NRA for their honesty. They are prepared to concede that *some* of the work they undertake is downright silly …

Yours etc.
John Quinn

P.S. My good friend and Roscrea native, the historian George Cunningham, later advised me that INANE is the local townland (pronounced EYE-NAAN) where the works are progressing. I still prefer my initial interpretation.

P.P.S. Also in Tipperary, I came across a well-drilling company truck which advertised the fact that one of its many services was 'Monitoring Bores' … What an interesting county is Tipperary!

Teacher

I BEGAN MY WORKING LIFE AS A TEACHER. I had always wanted to be a teacher. It seemed a noble calling. And it is. It is also hard work. There are days of drudgery but there are also diamond days – when a lesson catches fire, when a child who struggles with the written word suddenly produces a phrase or sentence that lifts your heart and lightens your step. Facing a huge class of very mixed ability was a daunting prospect.

In *The Master*, Bryan McMahon captures the challenging nature of teaching when he reflects on his first class in Listowel School …

'So there they were before me, merchants' sons with Little Duke shoes, poachers and sons of poachers, weavers of fiction, the cunning, the intelligent and the dull … The dutiful, the diligent, the ambitious, the lovable epileptic and the equally lovable Down's Syndrome child – all were there; the nervous and the fearless, the runaways, the nail-biters, the accident-prone, the superficially perfect, and the cross-grained. The "fixers", the precocious, the kickers, the chewers of putty and mortar, the thumb suckers … the sensitive, the nose-bleeders and the mitchers … the gifted, the unpredictable, the ungovernable … the prey-seekers, the informers, the impenetrable, the esoteric, the horse-lovers, the deaf.'

The Wee Hammer

MY UNCLE JOHN IN COUNTY MONAGHAN WAS a saddler by trade. It was one of the great delights of our childhood trips to that land of the wee hills to spend time with John in his workshop in the loft. What is it about lofts that makes them such intriguing places to visit? Access to this loft was by an external stone stairs, from the top of which one had views of distant Lake Muckno.

On entering the loft I was engulfed by the pervasive smell of leather. I loved that smell. I loved that loft. Ranged along John's bench was an assortment of tools – lasts, hammers, knives, awls, pincers – and scattered about were various works in progress – horses' collars, saddles, harness, boots (he was a cobbler too).

'Are you ready for work?' John would ask in his gentle, reassuring voice. 'I suppose you'll be wanting the wee hammer?' He reached for a small, light hammer which was perfect for a little boy. He then rooted around for some soft leather offcuts and a handful of brads (tiny nails). 'Off you go now!'

I was in heaven, earnestly imitating my mentor in making a leather 'piece'. The offer of the wee hammer was not just a pacifier on his part. It was his way of welcoming me into his world. We would engage in desultory conversation while we both 'worked'. I would be introduced to visiting farmers. Those were truly halcyon hours.

Uncle John died when I was thirteen. It was my first experience of a family death. I miss him still. I miss the loft and the entrancing smell of leather. And of course, the wee hammer.

Why?

IT'S SUCH AN INOFFENSIVE LITTLE WORD – one syllable, three letters – but what a thrill it must have been for each of us as children to master it and know its import. Here was the key to enlightenment, knowledge, understanding. Why is it dark? Why is the man sad? Why is everything? We proceeded to assail our parents relentlessly and they in turn did their best to satisfy our curiosity. Why was wonderful!

It did not remain so for all of us, however. As we grew older, curiosity took on darker shades. Older generations (sometimes, unpardonably, teachers) warned us that 'curiosity killed the cat'. A dangerous, bad thing, that curiosity. It could kill you. As a writer for children who visits schools, it never ceases to amaze me that twenty-first-century children have experienced this admonition. That, I tell them, is the greatest load of rubbish you will ever hear. To be a writer, to be human, to learn, you need to be curious.

Writers, artists, inventors are wonderful people! They are full of wonder. They wonder why? What if? So be curious like the old cat. It won't kill you!

It is curiosity, not caution, that will save the world. The great writer and broadcaster Studs Terkel – who lived into his nineties – knew that all too well. He left instructions that the following be carved on his tombstone –

CURIOSITY DIDN'T KILL THIS CAT

Bookmarks

THEY SERVE MUCH MORE THAN THEIR stated mundane purpose. For me there is no greater delight than in opening a book from my shelves and coming across an improvised bookmark – a postcard, a child's drawing, even a bus ticket. I have just come across the latter in a collection of Pat Ingoldsby's prose. It records a journey into work on the 84 bus on 5 January 1999. What preoccupied me on that day, I wonder. Did it turn out to be a good day? In the family bible there is a memento of an historic day – three specially printed bus tickets for the 'Visit of Pope John Paul II, 29 September 1979'. I remember the children's excitement at boarding a bus at five o'clock in the morning …

Elsewhere in the bible is Declan's (age 7) depiction of 'My Family – We Are the Quinns'. Five matchstick humans and a matchstick dog – and a heart inserted between Mum and Dad. From out of a Heaney collection tumbles a postcard from Lisa (age 9) who is on holiday with her granny in Galway. 'We have been to three churches already today … It is so hot, you could fry an egg on the pavement (*sketch of sizzling egg*) – if you had an egg …' And a final impassioned plea – 'DON'T LET JOANNA (*friend*) MAKE ANGEL DELIGHT!' (seemingly a previous effort had led to disaster …)

What memories such bookmarks conjure up! If I am honest, most of them were not bookmarks at all. I have a habit of slipping such mementoes randomly into books with the intention of happening upon them delightedly by chance many years hence. They are not bookmarks, but landmarks in a child's development, in the living of a life.

Longing for Home

THANKFULLY, I HAVE NEVER EXPERIENCED the pain of forced migration. As a writer, I can only try to imagine the migrant's sense of longing and loss. This is one such attempt from my novel, *Generations of the Moon*. It is 1926. Jimmy McCabe writes home from Philadelphia to his girlfriend Bridie.

Dear Bridie,

I know you think the worst of me for not writing, but it took me a long time to settle in here and to tell you the truth I doubt if I ever will. Give me Kerley's bog any day in preference to the busy streets of Philadelphia. This is one big country, Bridie – too big for my liking. There's all colours and creeds here and that's for sure. You should see the traffic in this city. I can tell you Pete McMahon's dog wouldn't sleep in the middle of the road like he does in Cullyboe!

The work is hard on the back but it's work and it's money. Give me five years and I'll be president of the railroad! Tell Pete I'm sorry the team lost the Feis Cup Final. They obviously missed me! D'ye mind the time the *Democrat* wrote about me – 'McCabe was industrious as ever and floated over two delightful minors …' I still have the cutting somewhere.

I suppose you think I'm having a brave wild time over here. To tell the truth, never a day goes by when I don't think of Cullyboe – and you. Little things – like the schoolhouse dance or the smell of the flax or sitting on McMahon's window after Mass. I look down that never-ending railway line and all I see is Cullyboe with its wee hills and fields. It's a terrible thing to be so far away from your own folk. Terrible. Remember me to all. Think of me sometimes.

Jimmy

An Aural Theatre

LISTENING TO *TODAY WITH PAT KENNY* ON the radio, I was particularly taken with a phrase used by Marie Louise O'Donnell, who was reporting from the National Ploughing Championships. The sounds she could hear were 'the aural theatre of my childhood'. A beautiful phrase. It set me thinking about what would constitute the aural theatre of my childhood …

The purr of the boiling kettle on the range … the music of milking as the warm fresh milk sprayed into the rising froth … the slice and suck of the slane in turfcutting action … the wheeze of blacksmith Bill Kelly's bellows and the ring of his anvil … the empty thwack of the wooden 'clappers' that replaced the altar bell during Holy Week … the chanting of multi-purpose tables at school – *eight sevens, fifty-six pence, four and eightpence* … the cheeping of day-old chicks in the aerated box that came on the Ballina bus … the church clock counting the hours through the night … the raucous concert of crows settling for the night in the Protestant church grounds … 'I taut I taw a puddy-tat' sung by Sylvester and Tweety-pie on the radio … 'Tantum Ergo' sung at Benediction … Ian Priestley Mitchell on the Hospitals' Sweepstakes programme saying 'Goodnight, everyone, goodnight' …

The Angel in the Green

I HAVE WRITTEN ABOUT THIS 'MOMENT' elsewhere but it is a major transformative event in my life and so deserves inclusion here.

August 2001. I am slowly and painfully coming to terms with the sudden death of my wife Olive six weeks earlier. I take a bus into O'Connell Street, Dublin, clutching an album of photographs I have assembled from our thirty-five-year relationship. I purchase a book in Eason's, and because it is a lovely summer afternoon, I decide to walk back to RTÉ. On the way I pause to rest in St Stephen's Green, light a cigar and flick through my album. Three 'winos' are sprawled on the grass before me. One approaches me (why did I stop here?) – 'Any chance of an ould cigar, boss?' I offer him one, hoping he will go away but instead he sits beside me and we puff away.

He is articulate and witty and not in any way offensive. He tells me his life-story. A successful jockey in his youth, who ultimately 'held' a few horses on their owners' instructions. He was brought before the Turf Club and had his licence revoked. Everything went downhill from there – unemployment, alcoholism, marriage break-up, wife and children leave. And now here he was, homeless, alcoholic. I think – there but for the grace of God … A few wrong decisions and life falls apart. I enjoy his company.

Cigars finished, I stand up to go and for some reason tell him my story in one sentence: 'My wife died six weeks ago.' He puts his arms around me, whispers in my ear: 'The seed in your heart shall blossom', and returns to his friends. The pure poetry of his words stuns me. I turn to wave goodbye to him. He mimes that poetic statement.

A week later, when I recount this meeting to John O'Donohue, his reaction was immediate. 'That was an angel, a messenger.'

Thank you, Olive.

Mad Cow

THERE WAS GREAT EXCITEMENT IN ENNIS yesterday. A cow that was being unloaded from a cattle-box at the local mart suddenly became very agitated and broke free, charging wildly through the streets. A few brave souls tried to stop her but she ran them down. Thankfully, no one was seriously injured. The cow, even more agitated, ran blindly through the streets until a group of farmers managed to herd her into a field. Even then she broke through a gate into another field where she eventually rested, though still clearly distressed.

A wise farmer gave his interpretation of the event. 'That cow was used to one person all her life – the farmer that owned her. She went wild because she was handled by people who didn't know how to handle her. It was all new to her and she got spooked.' Another added, 'She was probably never in a box before in her life and had only ever been between fields.'

It all made good column inches and video footage of course, but what terror must have coursed through that poor beast – terror at the strange and unfamiliar. Over twenty-four hours later she is still distressed in a strange field. Her owner will attempt to bring her home today. I hope he succeeds. She needs the familiarity of her own fields. For now, in the field where she is contained, the carcass of a dead calf lies beside a bush. The ultimate price of terror and distress.

The Ring

IT IS A PLAIN GOLD BAND.

I remember having it engraved *Haec Olim Meminisse Iuvabi*t – One day it will delight us to remember these things – in memory of the wonderful evening when I fell in love with Olive walking through the woods in a TB sanatorium.

I remember slipping it on her finger on a September day two years after that woodland walk.

I remember it always being there on that finger no matter how hard life could buffet us.

I remember the June evening when she died. The nurse in the mortuary handed me a packet containing 'two yellow rings and a yellow necklace … '

I remember taking that wedding ring to a jeweller who suggested splitting it and enlarging it to fit my own finger. No! You can't split it!

Instead I bought a gold chain to wear the ring around my neck.

It is the most incredible source of comfort to fondle it and kiss it, especially when life buffets you really hard.

It is a plain gold band.

Haec olim meminisse iuvabit.

At Play

I LOVE TO WATCH AND LISTEN TO CHILDREN at play. We once lived next door to a playschool and one of the daily delights was to hear the laughter and gabble of the children when they were allowed out to play in the garden.

The great educationist Friedrich Froebel wrote:

> Play is the highest phase of child development. It gives joy, freedom, contentment, inner and outer rest, peace with the world. It holds the source of all that is good.

I was passing our local school the other day. It was lunchtime so I stopped to watch the children at play. Such abandon! Such happiness! In the middle of it all, a football match. Surging, swerving bodies. Shrieks of joy. Howls of disappointment. Elsewhere a chain of six swoops and swirls in pursuit of another link. In a corner two close pals are seated on the grass in earnest conversation. Three others are searching animatedly among the bushes. A lone boy is seated against the wall, looking thoughtful. A girl joins him. A line of children waits patiently for a turn at skipping, chanting as they wait. Others wander about in little knots, avoiding careering bodies that seem certain to collide but never do.

The bell rings and slowly the crazy circus of delight dissolves into regimented lines and order returns. I walk away, tempted to play hopscotch on the pavement squares, but someone may be watching.

Dogger

IT HAPPENS SO OFTEN. YOU GO IN SEARCH OF a particular book and your attention is diverted by another that you haven't looked at for years. It happened again recently when, in pursuit of a much more serious tome, I came across a children's book – much-creased, occasionally stained and seriously frayed at the edges, but still intact after thirty years. *Dogger* by Shirley Hughes. A modern children's classic – the universal tale of a greatly loved toy that goes missing. In this instance, a worn-out, very old, flop-eared dog called Dogger, who belonged to Dave. Ah, Dogger ...

I first read *Dogger* to our son Declan when he was five – the first of 579 readings, or so it seems. Declan became as attached to the book as Dave was to Dogger. Again and again he would demand it as a bedtime story, to the point where he (and I) must have known it off by heart. Consequently, I could never take a shortcut – 'You left out where he looked under the stairs ...' It was, I suppose, the reassurance of the familiar – and it was that special moment of warmth when father and son were united in a unique way, a 'little island in the day', as a psychologist once described it to me.

Of course there was a happy ending for the distraught Dave and all was well – every night – for the devoted Declan. He's a thirty-something now, but I hope he remembers those 'islands'. Leafing through Shirley Hughes' beautiful book, I certainly do, with no little warmth.

A Handy Moment 1 – The Struggle

CHARLES HANDY IS A SOCIAL PHILOSOPHER whose writings and broadcasts on such issues as the future of work, fulfilment, the philosophy of enough, etc. have been internationally acclaimed. Over a period of twenty-five years as contributor to my radio programmes and as a friend and mentor, he has created many moments of insight and inspiration for me. Here are just a few of them from 'An Evening with Charles Handy', recorded in Dublin in 1996.

'Teresa of Avila was a sixteenth-century Spanish holy woman. She was both a Christian saint and a Jewish woman but they could cope with that in those times! Once on a journey she had to cross a river in spate with her companions. They gathered up their skirts and fought their way across. Reaching the far bank, exhausted and ill, she cried out to the Lord, "Lord, why do you do this to me?"

'And He said – "I do this to test those that love Me."

'She replied – "No wonder, Lord, they are so few!"

'The moral of the story for me is that life is meant to be a struggle. You do not fully understand yourself, develop yourself, fulfil yourself, live up to what your Creator intended you to be, unless you struggle through the tests that life sets you.

'Can we imagine what life would be like if there were no difficulties? For a start, you would be pretty damn boring! Of course we need help to cross the river, whether that be in the form of prayer or whatever, but we should rejoice in the choices before us. Otherwise life would be very bland.'

A Handy Moment 2 – The White Stone

'THERE IS A MYSTERY AT THE HEART OF things. What is it all for? What is life all about? I am drawn to a peculiar verse from the Book of Revelation:

> To anyone who prevails, the Spirit says, I will give a white stone on which is written a new name which no one knows except he who receives it. (Rev 2:17)

'What does it mean? I think it means that if you prevail, beyond uncertainty and doubt, you will know who you really are and will have earned your white stone. So many people never get to that point. They are the victims of an organisation, a boss, a family. It is said that by the time you die, you will only have learned a quarter of what you are capable of knowing. We have a need of something bigger than ourselves, a need to contribute, to leave a mark, to make a difference. That is what will earn for us the white stone which will tell us who we are and what we are for.

'The poet Keats wrote about *negative capability* – the capability to withstand uncertainty and doubt and still be yourself. "Truth is beauty," he wrote. And truth will set you free. Some would call what he argued for as faith. He called it negative capability. Names do not matter. Earning the white stone does.'

A Handy Moment 3 – Enough

'I AM VERY INTRIGUED BY THE PHILOSOPHY of enough. There is an old theology which says, "You can't know abundance until you have defined what is enough."

'What is enough in terms of achievement, success, money? Where does it end? Ireland's economy is currently growing at the rate of 6 per cent per annum [this was in 1996]. Faster than most OECD countries. Faster than Singapore! Brilliant! But where does it stop? If you continue at this rate, in a hundred years' time you will consume thirty-two times as much as now – thirty-two times more cars, televisions, McDonald's … And in the process, as has happened everywhere else, 80 per cent of the wealth will go to 20 per cent of the people. When that happens, it makes me wonder if capitalism can ever be compatible with democracy. When is enough enough? When does it stop? When do we say, let's spend more here and less there so that there can be a more decent life for all? When will organisations stop growing and growing until they dismember themselves?

'I would love a society which could define enough as Aristotle did, with his concept of the *golden mean*. Wealth to him was not good or bad, as long as it was viewed as a means to something greater.'

(A note from 2011 – were those words prophetic or what?)

A Letter to the Editor 2

Stradbally North
Clarinbridge

20 January 2007

The Editor
The Irish Times
Dublin 2

Dear Madam,

How positively regal Maeve Binchy looks in your wonderful photograph on page one of today's *Irish Times*! Should we ever give up the republic (and all the auld sins that go with it) and opt for a monarchy instead, Maeve would be an eminently suitable choice to rule over us. After all, Queen Maeve has an authentic ring to it …

Just think. She could have her beloved Gordon as her very own Poet Laureate. And for a Council of State she could have her very own Circle of Friends …

How about it, Ma'am? You could even live on Tara Road …

Yours in anticipation,
John Quinn

In Paradiso

FILM PRODUCER DONAL HAUGHEY WANTED to make a documentary based on my childhood memoir, *Goodnight Ballivor, I'll Sleep in Trim*, so we went to the County Meath village on a reconnoitering mission. One of the locations we visited was Sherrock's Garage, which on freezing Sunday nights in my childhood was our local cinema where Siki Dunne would put on a picture show.

I had not set foot in the garage for over fifty years, but when Robert Sherrock opened that door, he unlocked a treasury of memories. It was like stepping into a time warp. The interior was exactly as I had remembered it. The stout, scarred and worn workbench along one wall. Boxes of rusting tools, a jar of washers and nuts. A solid vice affixed to the bench. Castrol oil-drums propped against the opposite wall. An uneven oil-pocked floor. Old tyres strewn about. Apart from a stack of turf at the rear, nothing had changed. Everywhere the faint smell of oil and grease.

I had only to close my eyes and the turf-stack dissolved into the raised, expensive (two shilling) benches at the rear. I was on a lower wooden (one shilling) bench towards the front. The great sliding doors were draped in a huge white sheet and on that sheet Jimmy Cagney played out his final moments. Gunshots echoed in the rafters. I gripped the wooden bench as Cagney's evil cackle froze me to the sawdust floor. And then that deranged boast:

'Made it, Ma! Top of the world!'

Sandra

THE SUMMER OF 1956 WAS NOT A HAPPY ONE for me. At fourteen years of age I had been devastated by the news of Grace Kelly's wedding to Prince Rainier. Surely she knew of my undying love for her – and now she weds HIM! I struggled through my Inter Cert exam. During the summer holidays I went down to Fitzwilliam Tennis Club in Dublin to watch the Irish Open Championships. And there (on the rebound) I fell in love with Sandra Reynolds, who was tall and slim and simply beautiful, her graceful movement like the gazelle of her native South Africa … Life was suddenly bright again.

When Sandra played Wimbledon the following year, I wrote to her – but no doubt she had a busy schedule … That schedule included a return to Ireland where she won both the Irish Open and the South of Ireland Open in Limerick. I watched her every stroke, but could not bring myself to tell her of my love. Another rejection would be just too much.

I did tell the world, however, thirty-five years later, in a radio documentary on my boarding-school days … 'He loved Sandra Reynolds. Together they would be happy forever – even when they had retired after winning the Wimbledon Mixed Doubles title for a record sixth successive time …'

And now we move to 2007. An enterprising Limerick tennis veteran, Ivan O'Riordan, manages to bring Sandra (and her husband!) back to Limerick to celebrate the Golden Jubilee of her South of Ireland win. And he invites me also to meet my heroine. Oh joy! Oh rapture! To meet her face to face, especially after having the documentary excerpt played in public! She was charming, graceful and elegant as ever. Just shows you. Dreams can come true – even after fifty years.

Cloneycavan Man

THE PRESERVATIVE POWERS OF THE BOG were in evidence a few years ago when Cloneycavan Bog (a few miles from where I grew up in Ballivor, Co. Meath) gave up the body of a young man who had met a violent end some two thousand years ago. I went to see Cloneycavan Man on display in the National Museum …

I wonder who you are, Cloneycavan Man. Might you be a Douglas or a Murray? I went to school with Sean Murray from Cloneycavan … They say you came to a bad end. I hope you didn't suffer too much … A local wag suggested you might have been the victim of a nasty Feis Cup football match: 'Them Ballinabrackey fellas are notorious' … But seriously, I am curious about you. How was life for you all those years ago? Hard, I'm sure. Brutal. Cold. Damp. Scraping around for food. Did you keep a beast or two? Maybe that's why …

I see you wore hair gel. Bit of a man for the ladies, were you? Did you love someone? Maybe that's why … Hope you didn't have children. How they would have grieved for you. They say you might have been 'a sacrificial offering'. Not much consolation for your loved ones – seeing you hacked to death and thrown in a hole somewhere … And now here you are, given up by the bog two thousand years later. A specimen. On display. Thousands like me coming to peer at you … make jokes about you. And then? You'll probably be put back 'into storage' …

You're a neighbour's child, Cloneycavan Man. A proud Meath man who was literally dealt a hard blow. I'd love to take you from here and give you a proper burial in Kilaconnigan Cemetery, just up the road from Cloneycavan … No more a specimen … No more on display … Back home … At peace.

Birth of a Song

'THE FIRST TIME EVER I SAW YOUR FACE' IS one of the great modern love-songs, written by Ewan McColl for his wife Peggy Seeger. In 1987 I recorded a three-hour interview with the folk legends (in a B&B in Rathgar, Dublin), which became an award-winning series: 'Ewan and Peggy'. Naturally, I had to ask them about that song.

PEGGY: About 1956 I was on a sabbatical from Radcliffe College in the USA, trekking around Europe playing my music. I was in Denmark when I got a phone-call from London from folk music collector Alan Lomax. He needed a female singer/banjo player for a television series, *Dark of the Moon*. When I arrived in London he told me that he really needed me for a new singing group he was forming. I had been travelling for twenty-six hours and looked a mess in jeans. Alan's girlfriend, a posh model, literally scrubbed me clean, gave me one of her dresses, a fantastic hairdo, makeup and high heels, so when I tottered into the studio, that was the first time ever Ewan saw me … Poor Ewan fell in love with this vision.

EWAN: It wasn't the vision, it was the banjo!

PEGGY: About a year later I was on a solo tour in America and urgently needed new material – a love-song that would last one minute, twenty-five seconds! So Ewan wrote this song and sang it to me over the phone.

EWAN: The only time I ever sang it!

PEGGY: I remember writing it down because it was difficult to remember. It is almost classical folksong tradition – The first time … The first time … The first time – each verse taking the courtship further. It got instant reaction and became a huge hit and has been interpreted in many ways. But I hold that no one sings it as well as I do, because I understand it in a folksong manner. It's a simple lyric melody like an unaccompanied Irish song.

Uncle Jimmy

MY FATHER CAME FROM A SMALL FARM IN County Monaghan. It was our great thrill as children to be brought on summer Sunday trips from the flat Midlands to the wee hills of Monaghan and to be in the company of my father's siblings there. Gentle, soft-spoken, self-effacing people who nourished our childhood and the memory of whom continues to nourish me. None more so than Uncle Jimmy, a bachelor who lived all his four-score years in Drumacon, working the stony grey soil. I only have to read Patrick Kavanagh's 'Ploughman' –

> *I turn the lea-green down*
> *Gaily now,*
> *And paint the meadow brown*
> *With my plough.*
>
> *I dream with silvery gull*
> *And brazen crow.*
> *A thing that is beautiful*
> *I may know.*

> *Tranquillity walks with me*
> *And no care.*
> *O, the quiet ecstasy*
> *Like a prayer.*
>
> *I find a star-lovely art*
> *In a dark sod.*
> *Joy that is timeless! O heart*
> *That knows God!*

I close my eyes and I am walking the furrow with gentle, quiet Jimmy. And tranquillity walks with us both. And no care.

Easter Dawn

IN THE EARLY 1990S, JOHN O'DONOHUE initiated the practice of a Dawn Mass on Easter Sunday in the ruins of Corcomroe Abbey, the great twelfth-century Cistercian settlement in the Burren, Co. Clare. They were very special occasions, made so by John's intense connection with this sacred place and its beautiful natural setting.

We set off on the half-hour drive in the 'darkest hour before dawn'. As we approached Corcomroe valley, a constant stream of headlights pierced the gloom as the procession of cars snaked down the narrow road to the abbey. The congregation swelled in number – families with small children who were excited at being out in the dark, the local community and many who had travelled long distances to be here. A great buzz of conversation echoes through the ruin until a grey light filters over the Burren and the first twitterings of the unseen birds herald the Easter dawn.

John invites us to be silent so that we can dwell on the areas where we need Easter healing and hope. Mass begins with prayers and readings punctuated by slow airs from local musicians. And all the time the choral symphony of the birds provides the natural background music to this great celebration. John's homily is on the theme of our journey from darkness into light and he reminds us of the young man who braved the darkness of the human journey and carried it to Calvary. 'Let the new tender light of the Resurrection touch our fears and overcome them.' He blesses the four elements – air, earth, fire and water – before moving into the ruined abbey for the Consecration of the Mass. Again, intervals of music and silence.

The glorious light of Easter bathes us in warmth and welcome as we emerge from the abbey. Hallelujah! There's tea and buns for everyone and, as John puts it, 'a feast of reels' to send us home.

Farewell to John

THE SUDDEN DEATH OF JOHN O'DONOHUE IN 2008 at the age of fifty-two left a deep void in the hearts and minds of the many people for whom his writings, talks and broadcasts had done much to feed the 'unprecedented spiritual hunger' he had observed in modern society. His funeral in his beloved Fanore on a bitter January day was at once a lament for a lost leader and a celebration of a great mind. These lines are part of a longer poem, 'The Journey', I wrote on that day.

We were promised a hard frost
But overnight a milder wind
Blew in from Fanore
And so we drove down ice-free roads
Through Kinvara and Bellharbour
A golden Burren sunrise
Heralded what you called
The wonder of the arriving day.

We parked amid the caravans
And walked along the singing river

Remembering how you envied it
Carried by the surprise
of its own unfolding.

The obsequies began
Eucharistic mystery
Music and memory
And laughter, always laughter.

And so we filed past your coffin
And laid hands on it.
And no – we couldn't take it in.
We held your loved ones' hands
Wishing we could especially mind Josie
Proud and frail and broken.

And then the final, final stage
To Creggagh
A great caravan
Snaking along that wild
And surf-tossed shore
That thrilled you so.

A vicious south-easterly
Whipped us with icy rain
And stung us to tears
As we lowered you to lie
Face to face with rock
In a limestone valley
Your soul already freed
Face to face with God
On the eternal mountain.

Charlie Pigott played
Éamonn an Chnuic
As we huddled
Báite fuar fliuch
For the last farewell.

Home now
Through the dying day
Down flooding roads
Past sodden fields
With one more stop to make
At Corcomroe

To remember Easter dawns
When you blessed the elements
And sang the Risen Christ.

A silence
And then past
Weeping Burren flags
Descending
Through a shroud of mist
Into the dark.

Possibility

JUST SUPPOSE. IT IS THE BEGINNING OF THE academic year. Your class assembles for the first lecture. Enter the professor. 'Right,' he says. 'First thing – I'm giving each one of you an A!' Sharp collective intake of breath. Can this be true? 'Second thing.' Uh oh, here it comes. 'In the next two weeks, I want each of you to write me a letter, dated next May and beginning – "Dear Professor, I got my A because …"' The whole letter must be written in the past tense …' Just suppose.

This approach is for real and it was outlined for me by the man who practises it – Ben Zander, who is a professor of the New England Conservatory of Music. It is a very subtle and liberating approach. Zander wants to raise the students' self-esteem to see all of who they are and be all of who they are. They must 'see' all of the milestones and insights they will attain during that year. It is all about dreaming, about positivity, about possibility.

Drawing on Michelangelo's concept of releasing the statue from within the marble block by chipping away all that is not the statue, Zander argues that educators should be concerned with chipping away all that inhibits the child's development of skills and self-expression. Zander's approach 'would transport the teacher's relationship from the world of measurement into a universe of possibility'. And he argues this approach can be applied in any relationship or any walk of life.

Just suppose.

Márla-fied

DURING THE COURSE OF A WRITERS-IN-Schools visit, the school principal prevailed on me to pop into 'the wee ones' (infant classes) for a few minutes. I normally work with middle and upper standards but it is equally a joy to be with the wee ones as, wide-eyed with wonder, they put together a story about Kevin the Kangaroo, interspersed with personal revelations such as 'mammy is getting a new baby' or 'I have a loose tooth'.

It was in this particular infant classroom that a familiar aroma wafted me back to my own childhood days – the smell of plasticine, or *márla* as we called it. I tracked it down and besought its minder if I might borrow it – just to feel it again, squeeze it, roll it, shape it …

The next time I visit my grandchildren in London, I am going to bring with me a giant multipack (and multi-coloured pack) of plasticine. Oh yes, Eva and Georgia, I know you have Wiis and Nintendos and Barbies and all sorts of sophisticated toys, but wait till you see what you can do with plasticine … You just take a lump of it and squeeze it and squidge it and squirm it like this and pull it and press it and pinch it like that and look there's red and yellow and blue and then you roll it between your hands like that yes I'll let you have a go in a minute and the lovely smell it leaves and look you can make a dinosaur with the longest tail ever and bright yellow eyes like that and then you make a huge ball that's a dinosaur egg yeh in a minute I just want to see if it tastes the same …

A Walk Into History

I WOULD NOT NORMALLY WELCOME A 4:30 a.m. wake-up call but this was a very special call and a very special day. The month was September 2007 and the place was Jerusalem. I was on a pilgrimage from Galway to the Holy Land and already I had been awestruck by the reality of locations that hitherto had been but scriptural references – Gethsemane, Emmaus, the Mount of Olives. Today however was the special day. We would walk the *Via Dolorosa* – the Way of the Cross. As we left our base in Bethlehem at 5:00 a.m., there was already a long winding queue of Palestinians waiting to enter Jerusalem through the security gate …

At 5:45 a.m. the group began its walk through the twisting, smelly alleyways of Jerusalem. It was the perfect time to do the walk. The alleyways were quiet, peaceful and cool. We took turns in threes to carry a symbolic cross and I was privileged to read a reflection at the sixth station. It was a deeply uplifting moment and the whole experience was quite moving. We were in time for 7 a.m. Mass in the Church of the Holy Sepulchre, beside which was the reputed site of Golgotha, the scene of the Crucifixion. When you look at an artistic depiction of Golgotha, you easily forget that over two thousand years a huge city has grown up around that barren site.

Hence my having to crawl under a Greek Orthodox altar and reach through a hole in the ground to touch Golgotha. I was in touch with the ages. Finally we descended into the nearby tomb of Jesus. An extraordinary morning. An overwhelming experience.

An Old Photograph

IN AN AGE OF DIGITAL CAMERAS AND camera-phones, the notion of a photograph album is fast becoming obsolete. When photography was in its infancy however, a photograph album was a family treasure. I remember my mother's prized album. It had a beautiful ornate cover, resembling a monastic shrine of another age. Cameras were rare in my youth, so photographs were valued acquisitions. The visit of a returned Yank ensured several additions to the collection.

The album is long gone, its contents a jumbled memory of ghostlike figures from a black and white or sepia past, often unidentified. One photograph stays in my mind. A man riding away from the camera on his bicycle, with a little terrier trotting faithfully behind. It isn't much of a photograph, technically (subject too distant), but it is the caption on the reverse side that intrigues me: 'Heels Dunne on bicycle' ...

Who was Heels? How did he get that name? I never found out but fifty years later I re-created him as a minor character in my first children's novel, *The Summer of Lily and Esme*. Heels was one of a number of men crowded into the church porch who were shamed by the parish priest into filling the empty front pews. As he sheepishly made his way up the aisle, the steel tips on the heels of his boots rang out on the tiled floor. And so a name was born.

That was my version of his story. I hope Heels isn't too upset by it – but it is an example of how an innocent moment in time, recorded on a primitive camera and stored in a treasured album, can be the trigger for some interesting writing.

Rock of Ages

IT HAD LONG BEEN A DREAM OF MINE TO visit Skellig Rock and the dream was realised when I landed there in September 2000 to make a radio documentary. It was an exhilarating and wonderful experience, literally wonderful – full of wonder. These were my thoughts as I stood high on a cliff-top, seawash crashing beneath, gulls crying above.

'*Tá mé ag seasamh ar imeall an domhain.* I am standing at the edge of the world, or so it must have seemed to the men who dared to make this place their home, their place of penitence and prayer almost fifteen hundred years ago. I'm on Sceilg Mhichíl, this great fortress of rock standing proudly against the wild Atlantic waves, some eight miles off the southwest coast of Kerry. A wild, unimaginably beautiful place that for some five hundred years was a monastic settlement, the last outpost of Christianity in the then known world. It's a rugged, craggy, barren, dangerous place. It's a sacred place. The stones of the *cillíns* or beehive cells sing out stories of sacrifice and serenity, of deprivation and devotion. It's a truly humbling place – to find oneself a mere human speck on this great rock, which is in turn a mere fleck in the vastness of the Atlantic Ocean.

'I am overwhelmed, fearful and totally in awe of this wild, beautiful, sacred place. *Tá mé ar imeall an domhain*, on Skellig Rock off the southwest coast of Kerry.'

JOHN QUINN

Teaching Debut

IT IS INTRIGUING TO RECALL 'FIRSTS'. FIRST day at school. First girlfriend. First day at work. I began my working life as a teacher, so my first time in front of a class was a major moment in my life. I remember it clearly enough but I also have the benefit of the observations of another to bolster that memory.

As a student teacher in St Patrick's College of Education, my first teaching practice is with a class of forty-plus challenging ten year olds in the local model school in Drumcondra. As I take my first faltering steps, the class teacher, Stan O'Brien, sits at the bottom of the class. It is March 1960. I am eighteen years old and somewhat terrified …

Many years later somebody came across Stan's 'Observation Notes' for that day and sent them to me …

Exceedingly earnest in his approach, diligent in preparation, but his stern and stilted attitude precluded contact with his class and no amount of conscientiousness can overcome this lack. He must loosen up, present a less funereal countenance to the children [*boy, did my wife make hay out of* THAT!] and inject some humour into his teaching …

Of course you were right, Stan – but I WAS terrified! I think I have loosened up over the years but the memory of those first teaching days are still razor-sharp shards. There was a glimmer of hope, though, in the final sentence of Stan's report.

There was one faint ray – 'That was the first time the student smiled,' the children said.

Cows 1

I LOVE COWS.

I love the tranquilising effect of their doe-eyed gaze across a farm wall.

To behold them lying in the lush grass of a May meadow, chewing contentedly while rhythmically flicking their tails at nuisance flies – that is surely the essence of summer.

The poet James Reeves captures that scene thus:

Half the time they munched the grass
And all the time they lay
Down in the water-meadows
The lazy month of May,
A-chewing
A-mooing
To pass the hours away.

I love cows.

They are such placid and contented creatures. I love their easy, ambling gait, barrel-bellies full, swollen udders swaying as they make their way down a country road for evening milking. No one will rush them. Traffic can wait. They dictate the pace of life.

My father kept two cows. I have a memory of pulping mangolds for them on bitter winter evenings. I loved to stand between them in their stalls just to absorb the welcome heat of their bodies as they munched and chewed my offerings deliberately and contentedly.

I just love cows.

Cows 2

LIZZIE COYNE LOVED COWS TOO. AND SO DID her family. I know this because I am reading something Lizzie wrote over seventy years ago. It was part of the nationwide folklore collection project of 1937–38, when children in primary schools gathered folklore – customs, stories, trades and crafts, sayings – in their native parishes, and diligently wrote them into their copybooks which were then sent to the Irish Folklore Commission. The material is now stored in the Folklore Department 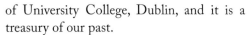 of University College, Dublin, and it is a treasury of our past.

Lizzie Coyne lived near Kinnegad and on 25 November 1938 she wrote, 'My father has nine cows. Their names are The Young Maoil, Blue Martin, Jim Murphy, The Old Kerry, Little Red, The White One, Little Black, Kinnegad Cow and Mrs Williams.'

Can't you just hear the nighttime conversation in the Coyne household?

> *That Little Red is a topper. She's milking great.*
> *The Old Kerry is off her food. I'm a bit worried about her.*
> *Can I have The White One's calf to rear?*

It's a long way from massive herds with anonymous yellow ear-tags.

A Double Blow

THIS MORNING'S RADIO NEWS BROUGHT SAD news on the double – the death in London of actor T. P. McKenna and in New York of pianist George Shearing, two entertainers who for over half a century have delighted me in their respective spheres.

I was privileged to interview T. P. a couple of times. I loved the rich sonority of his voice and how he could so easily switch to his original Cavan accent. We would exchange banter over Meath–Cavan football rivalry, but he was gracious to acknowledge that the people of Trim lodged a petition to the Ulster Bank to prevent him being moved to Dublin as he was 'invaluable to the town and its amusements' (the petition failed). He spoke so warmly of one of his heroes, Fr Vincent Kennedy of St Patrick's College, Cavan, who would invite T. P. and a few friends to his room for musical *soirées*, when Vincent would play on his Bechstein, give classes in music education and listen to the BBC Proms. This stylish and sophisticated man was a huge influence on the would-be actor. I later 'borrowed' him to become an important character in my novel, *Generations of the Moon*, and T. P. approved.

I write this while listening to George Shearing's 'I'll Remember April'. This London-born pianist, blind from birth, had a uniquely distinctive and delicate style as a jazz pianist, a style which thrilled audiences worldwide. I genuinely believe that anyone who enriches the lives of others so much with their talent must have a special place in heaven. Now in one dark morning's news I learn that both talents are stilled – the street footballer from Mullagh and the blind boy from Battersea – but there are so many moments of light to cherish.

Bobby

WE HAD A DOG AT MASS TODAY. NOT YOUR usual mischievous mutt that saunters up the aisle and into the sanctuary, defying all the altar-boys' embarrassing attempts to capture him. No, this dog was a guest of honour, publicly welcomed by Fr Dermody. His name is Bobby and the occasion was the funeral of his much-loved mistress, Rosemary Kennedy.

Rosemary was a writer, artist, dancer, and dog-lover. At the end of Mass, Mark Greene read out Bobby's story, as written by Rosemary. He had been abandoned in a nearby town some years earlier and was discovered by Rosemary when he was hanging out outside a supermarket in the hope of picking up some food scraps. Bobby's is an 'allsorts' pedigree. His tail, of which he is very proud, is definitely Pomeranian and he has a lovely tan and white colouring. Rosemary adopted him and the pair became inseparable, particularly on their riverside walks and most importantly in latter years when Rosemary bravely fought cancer.

So when Rosemary died this week, it was only right and fitting that Bobby attend her funeral and be publicly acknowledged for the important part he played in her life. He was of course impeccably behaved at Mass, though part of that may be the beginnings of his sense of loss. And when one of the mourners carried him out of the church behind Rosemary's coffin, we instinctively reached out to pet him, for he was a mourner too.

The Voice

I GREW UP IN THE RADIO ERA. ONE OF THE family's great delights was listening to the weekly episode of *The Foley Family* – the daily life of an ordinary Dublin household. Head of that household was Tom Foley, a much put-upon, misunderstood man who had to endure the humours of his wife Alice, the mischief of his son Brendan and the follies and foibles of his workmates and neighbours. Poor Tom! We had nothing but sympathy for this stout, barrel-chested 'Dub' (as I pictured him) as he railed against the world.

Little did I realise that a quarter of a century later I would come to work in the world of radio and would have the privilege of working with the members of the RTÉ Repertory Company. These included Pegg Monahan (who had played Alice Foley), who became a dear friend, and George Greene who had played Tom Foley. What a surprise lay in store for me there! George was no 'stout, barrel-chested Dub', but a tiny, wizened man racked with arthritis. Meeting him was a salutary lesson. The power of radio. The power of the voice.

Pigs

'MY NAME IS MICKEY SHERIDAN AND I'VE been in pigs all me life and all before me too.' Thus did pig-farmer Mickey introduce himself in a radio documentary of mine (2000). It was called *Pighomage* and it was my attempt to celebrate the pig and right wrongs done to that noble animal. Let's face it, the pig gets a bad press – 'the manners of a pig', 'pig-ignorant', 'the place is like a pig-sty', 'chauvinist pig' – the list goes on. Mickey Sheridan and his wife Gertie would have none of that.

When Mickey grew up in inner Dublin, nearly every house in the neighbourhood kept a pig or two, feeding it on domestic swill. But that was another era and now Mickey and Gertie run their little pig-farm at the foot of the Dublin mountains. Mickey introduces me to his sow Rosie. His affection for Rosie is evident. 'What is it, Rosie? What's wrong, girl? They love you to talk to them. And they love an auld scratch. Don't you, Rosie? Oh

indeed you do! D'ye hear her talking away to me? Oh she's a lovely girl, is our Rosie. My father always said you'd never see a pig in a circus because you could never train them to do anything – only sleep and eat …'

Gertie adds her defence. 'People think pigs are dirty, but they're not. They won't soil their bedding – they will wee in one corner and manure in another. They only roll in the muck to prevent them getting sunburn … They're very intelligent really. They don't eat everything – they don't like parsnips and onions for example. If they find a spoon, say, in the swill, they will play with it all day.'

Mickey gives Rosie a playful slap. 'How and ever, even the best of friends must part, no matter how long they've been knocking around … Isn't that right, my lovely girl?'

The Lure of Letters 1

I GOT A LETTER IN THE POST TODAY. IT IS A source of unfailing pleasure and of no small wonder to hear that familiar 'plat' as the letter tumbles through the letterbox. This particular one has come from Co. Wexford. The writer has enjoyed reading my childhood memoir and goes on to illustrate how my story resonates with hers. I savour each word. Letters have always been a major part of my life, whether as a homesick student at boarding school or a lovesick young man parted from his lover, whether as a friend or a parent. A letter needs time devoted to it – and effort. Someone took the time and trouble to procure pen and paper, to formulate thoughts, to create pictures, and then to make their way to a post office to dispatch that creation. A letter is personal and intimate. Someone cares. Someone understands, someone is troubled. Long live the letter!

Today in the age of electronic mail, the letter is touching *passé*, I suppose. And they call it 'snail mail'. I don't know about that. When I consider the concerted effort required from yesterday afternoon when my friend popped her letter in a postbox in Wexford – the handling, the sorting, the carrying by vans and trains – until Postman Pat (for that is his name) slipped it into my letterbox this morning, a snail does not come to mind. To travel all that distance within a day and be delivered into my hand for a paltry fifty-five cent is to me still a cause of wonder and delight. The pages are real in my hand, the handwriting distinctive, the sentiments uniquely personal. I am truly honoured.

JOHN QUINN

The Lure of Letters 2

I AM THANKFUL THAT I GREW UP AND courted in the age of the written letter, before the days of instant communication through text and email. From the moment I first laid eyes on the love of my life in a TB sanatorium, I wooed and thankfully won Olive McKeever by letter. For two years I wrote to her almost daily to ease the pain of our separation! Little wonder then that on the morning of our wedding a letter lay waiting for her.

My darling,

I know you won't have the time or powers of concentration to read mail on your wedding morning, but maybe you will spare a minute for a faithful correspondent of the last two and a half years!

The only reason I write is to give you a little giggle, to ease the tension, to make you happy – which is of course why I want you to accompany me down the aisle this morning.

I'd look a right eejit there on my own, wouldn't I? (P.S. You will turn up, won't you?)

I know more than anyone else how much you have gone through and I admire and love you madly for it. So these last few hours must not upset you. I'm with you every moment and I'm going to be the proudest man there is to take you from your father after those forty-three paces up the aisle (I've counted them!).

This is your day, my darling. Sail through it with all the radiance that only you can show. This is the day we dreamed of – let us live that dream. Me loves you, my beautiful one. This is a historic missive – my last to you in our single state. We've come a long way, pet, but from here on the way is pleasant and paved with love. Come to me, my darling. Come.

John x

The Lure of Letters 3

IF THE LETTER EVER BECOMES EXTINCT, IT will be a great loss to historians, who for centuries have drawn on letters as an archive source in recording social and political change. The personal letter shines a light on the lived life as no other document does. The following letter was written from the trenches at Ypres weeks before his death by the poet-soldier Francis Ledwidge to his friend, the writer Katharine Tynan. It conveys movingly both the stark horror of war and the homesickness of a lost young dreamer.

'We have just returned from the line after an unusually long time. It was very exciting this time, as we had to contend with gas, lachrymatory shells, and other devices new and horrible. It will be worse soon. The camp we are in at present might be in Tír na nÓg, it is pitched among such splendours. There is barley and rye just entering harvest days of gold, and meadowsweet rippling, and where a little inn named *In Den Neerloop* holds its gable up to the swallows, bluebells and goldilocks swing their splendid censers …

'I daresay you have left Meath and are back again in the brown wilds of Connaught. I would give one hundred pounds for two days in Ireland, with nothing to do but ramble from one delight to another … I want to see again my wonderful mother and to walk by the Boyne to Crewbawn and up through the brown and grey rocks of Crocknaharna. You have no idea of how I suffer with this longing for the swish of the reeds at Slane and the voices that I used to hear coming over the low hills of Currabwee …

'It is midnight now and the glow-worms are out. It is quiet in camp but the far night is loud with our guns bombarding the positions we must soon fight for.'

Bhutan

NOVEMBER 2008. THERE'S A WONDERFULLY exotic photograph in today's *Irish Times* of the newly crowned King of Bhutan in his throne room in the royal palace in the capital, Thimphu. His name is Jigme Khesar Namgyel Wangchuck – a namedropper's delight, surely. What really caught my eye in the accompanying report was the new king's pledge to maintain his father's 'unique philosophy of enhancing [his] country's Gross National Happiness, the singular barometer of the country's well-being that balances spiritual with material values.'

Gross National Happiness. Now, there's a concept! It was coined by King Jigme's dad (Jigme Singye Wangchuck to you) as long ago as 1972, when he declared Gross National Happiness more important than Gross Domestic Product and committed himself to building an economy to serve Bhutan's culture, based on Buddhist spiritual values. It was a brave move by the then ruler

of this tiny country (population 700,000) which is wedged in between giant neighbours India and China. And it wasn't idle talk. The concept is built on four pillars – the promotion of sustainable development, the preservation and promotion of cultural values, the conservation of the natural environment and the establishment of good governance. King Jigme Snr abdicated in 2006 and switched to democracy, leaving the new king with limited powers.

GNH. Would it work here? Should we invite Jigme over? I can already hear the murmur of dissent – like the Kerryman who greeted the introduction of decimal currency with the words: 'Sure, 'twill never catch on here.'

A Twenty-Cent Treasure

MY FRIEND AND FORMER RADIO COLLEAGUE, Tim Lehane, has an eye for books and bargains. Both came together recently when he wandered into Deansgrange Library and perused their 'Books for Sale – Withdrawn from Stock'. For twenty cent he picked up a copy of *I Saw Esau*, a collection of traditional children's rhymes by Iona and Peter Opie. Twenty cent! A hardback in mint condition. With illustrations by the wonderful Maurice Sendak. Twenty cent! And he bought it for *me*!

I saw Esau kissing Kate
The fact is we all three saw;
For I saw him,
And he saw me,
And she saw I saw Esau.

How I treasure this gift! I regularly laugh my way through it. In her Introduction, Iona Opie writes:

The best antidote to the anxieties and disasters of life is laughter, and this children seem to understand almost as soon as they are born. If laughter is lacking, they create it; if it is offered to them they relish it … We find we are born, so we might as well stay and do as well as we can, and while we are here we can at least enjoy the endearing absurdities of mankind.

I asked my mother for fifty cents
To see the elephant jump the fence;
He jumped so high he reached the sky
And didn't come back till the Fourth of July.

Me? I saw him jump for just twenty cent. Thank you, Tim.

Boarding

I SPENT FIVE YEARS OF MY LIFE IN BOARDING school. It is over fifty years ago now but the memories remain – the food, the winter cold and the longing for home, yes, but also the friendships, the kindnesses and a love of Latin! Seamus Heaney captures the boarding-school experience so well in this prose poem which he submitted to me for a fundraising book of school memories, *Must Try Harder.*

'I could make a book of hours of those six years, a Flemish calendar of rite and pastime set on a walled hill. Look – there is a hillside cemetery behind us and across the river the plough is going in a field and in between we are cloistered up against the gated town. Here, an obedient clerk kisses a bishop's ring; here is a frieze of seasonal games and here the assiduous illuminator bows himself to his narrow desk.

'In the study hall my hand was cold as a scribe's in winter. The supervisor rustled past, sibilant, vapouring into his breviary, his welted brogues unexpectedly secular beneath the hemmed soutane. Now I bisected the line AB, now found my foothold in a main verb in Livy. From my dormitory after lights-out, I revised the constellations and in the morning broke the ice on a water-jug with exhilarated self-regard.

'Champion of the hour, I clamped my bookish visor down, lowered my lance and galloped, terror-stricken, towards the exam lists.'

The Library of Friends

I WENT TO THE OPENING OF A LIBRARY yesterday. It was in the village of Corrandulla in County Galway. The village community called it *Leabharlann na gCáirde*, the Library of Friends. It commemorated the life of one of their own, Sally Hardiman, who died in 2009 and who was a member of a book circle.

Following Sally's death, a committee was set up to honour her. What better way than with a community library? A parish survey assessed the level of interest in such a venture. The community council offered the use of a room in the old girls' school. Fundraising ventures got under way. A 'book-drop' was organised, inviting people to donate unwanted books. Thousands of books were gifted. Galway County Library promised a 'top-up' of books which could be rotated regularly. The room was renovated, beautiful shelving was installed, a computer system was set up to log the books and a team of volunteers was recruited to run the library. All that remained was to find a name for the Library. The obvious one emerged – *Leabharlann na gCáirde.*

And so on a bitter December afternoon with dangerous icy roads everywhere, a huge crowd assembled to celebrate this remarkable venture – a library of some four thousand volumes assembled, housed and run by a small rural community. No wonder the committee members beamed with pride as they plied us with tea and mince pies – and a total love of books.

The Goal

THE MEATH–DUBLIN FOOTBALL SAGA IN THE summer of 1991 caught the imagination of the sporting public, not so much for its brilliant football but for its unrelenting intensity and passion. Four games – two with extra time – between these fierce rivals, until after five hours and forty minutes Meath emerged winners by a point. As a Meath man I have to declare a bias here, but let me recall the last couple of minutes of the final game.

Meath are three points down and seemingly out. Martin O'Connell retrieves the ball on his own end line and gives it to Mick Lyons. On to Mattie McCabe. A slick lay-off to Liam Harnan. He to Colm O'Rourke who is fouled and takes a quick free to 'Jinksy' Beggy. He gives it to Kevin Foley who passes it to P. J. Gillic and keeps running. Gillic to Tommy Dowd who passes it to O'Rourke and runs on to take the return pass and give it to the in-rushing Foley. Goal! Eleven passes and not one Dublin player had touched the ball!

No wonder it was voted the all-time greatest goal on television. And Kevin Foley was a corner-back who never scored anything previously or subsequently for Meath! To compound Dublin's misery, Meath won possession of the kickout and 'Jinksy' lashed over the winning point for Meath. Game over. Delight for Meath. Devastation for Dublin.

Sometimes in the dark of winter, when I am feeling low or bored, I reach for a videotape. *Dublin–Meath 1991*. Insert. Play. Enjoy.

Streetwise

MICHAEL IS OUR LOCAL STREET-SWEEPER. Twice a week, in all weathers, he removes the detritus of village life from our pathways, gulleys and corners in his handcart, wearing his high-visibility waistcoat which his County Council colleagues have inscribed with his 'licence plate' – 10 G MM. He is fastidious in his work and does much to enhance the appearance of our village, despite the efforts of many to do the opposite. He lives alone and in his spare time he loves to tinker with and repair old machines.

Above all else, Michael loves to meet people and talk to them as he works his way up and down the village. He has a witty turn of phrase and he brightens our lives in more senses than one. While discussing the perilous state of the economy with me recently he made a very wise observation – ''Tis verra hard to keep the bubble between the lines,' a reference to the bricklayer's spirit level.

How many of our pundits and experts could match that pearl of wisdom?

JOHN QUINN

The Best Medicine

THERE USED TO BE A FEATURE IN THE *Reader's Digest* called 'Laughter – The Best Medicine'. I found this to be true when I was hospitalised in Galway in 2006. One of my wardmates was a Connemara man who had worked on building sites in London. He loved to regale us with stories from those days. Two will suffice here.

In London, he claimed, you had to look after your property carefully or it might disappear. If you had your own shovel, for example, you never left it out of your sight. 'Indeed, there was one fellow I remember who used to bring his wheelbarrow home on the tube every evening ...' Even now I laugh at the incongruity of it all. *Mind the gap! Never mind the gap! Mind the wheelbarrow!*

'This other fellow had his own jackhammer. Every morning he'd start it up before he left for work, to ensure it was in working order. He had an upstairs flat and unfortunately one morning when he started up the jackhammer he lost control of it and it went through the floor and into the flat below!' There are kinder ways of being woken up.

I hope the Connemara man knows how much he contributed to my recovery to health.

Naming the Fields

ON A TRAIN JOURNEY THE PATTERN OF THE fields that whizz by always intrigues me. Who decided on their boundaries and why this or that particular pattern? And where did some fields get their names? In the 1937 Schools Folklore Collection, the children of Ballivor recorded the following fieldnames: The Duck Walk, The Pigeon Meadow, The Roughins, The Ruadháns, The Skunavans, The Carrigeen, The Fossocks, The Currachs, The Cretins (!), The Hawk's Island, Cluincín, The Bawn, The Pound Field, Cnoc Suibhne.

The origins of many of them are obvious but others could be the stuff of drama to rival John B. Keane. The Pound Field might be a field for impounding animals – or it might once have been sold for a pound. And if so, why … ?

O the grip, O the grip of irregular fields! No man escapes.

–PATRICK KAVANAGH,
'The Great Hunger'

November

WHO LIKES NOVEMBER? NOT ME. GREY DAYS of shrinking light. Leaden skies, mist and damp that seeps into your bones. The trees are:

> *... bare ruined choirs*
> *Where late the sweet birds sang ...*

On top of all that, November is *mí na marbh*, the month of the dead, when we feel loss more acutely. Not a cheering month. For me it brings a sense of foreboding.

November 1965 stands out in my personal history. I was diagnosed as having TB and was 'sentenced' to nine months of rest and recuperation in a sanatorium. I was a teacher in my mid-twenties, studying at night, full of visions and dreams. The world was my oyster. And now – disaster. On that first foggy, dank evening in my new surroundings it seemed that the sun might never break through again.

But of course it did. Four months later I met a fellow-patient – a stunningly elegant woman, a vision in a black leather coat. Her name was Olive. Smitten to the core, I wrote to her. She wrote back. A correspondence became a friendship. On a glorious May evening we daringly went for a walk in the woods. A friendship became love. We married two years later. For every November, there is a May.

In the Barrack Garden

I WAS BORN AND GREW UP IN THE VILLAGE OF Ballivor, Co. Meath, where my father was the local garda sergeant. When he retired we moved to Dublin, but those first thirteen years of my life in Ballivor had a profound effect on my formation. Over fifty years later, television producer Donal Haughey brought me back to Ballivor to film a documentary based on my childhood memoir, *Goodnight Ballivor, I'll Sleep in Trim.*

They were emotion-filled days, returning to scenes of my childhood, notably to the now-derelict house where I was born. But the most emotional return of all was to the garden of the garda barracks. It was quite a sizeable garden, every square inch of which was cultivated by my father. He had grown up on a small farm in County Monaghan and was never happier than when working the soil. I was his acolyte on those distant summer evenings – listening, watching, learning. My father was a quiet man, not overly demonstrative, but he was

there and I was happy to be in his company, serving my apprenticeship. He would chide me gently for overloading a barrow: 'That's the lazy man's load.'

I sat on a grassy bank while producer and cameraman discussed the next 'take'. But I could only hear the gentle coaxing of my father guiding horse and plough, only feel in my hand the wriggle of a worm rescued from the new-sliced soil. My heart welled up with gratitude, longing and love for that gentle, quiet man. As Seamus Heaney wrote about peeling potatoes with his mother, we were

… never closer the whole rest of our lives.

Leaving Otterbrook

LEAVING A FAMILY HOME FOR THE LAST TIME is an emotion-filled experience. Life in all its guises has been contained within those four walls. Memories flit between nooks and crannies. Voices echo down hallways and through the stairwell. There have been happy days you cherish and darker days you would wish to forget. Days and nights of joy and laughter. Days and nights of hurt and silence. Life in all its guises.

For fourteen years, we had lived in 'Otterbrook', a two-storey thatched house on a boreen leading to an inlet of Galway Bay. But now Olive was dead and it was time to move – to a smaller house which would be nearer to shops and services. So on a July afternoon in 2006 I said goodbye to 'Otterbrook'. I walked through each room, sifting its memories, noting for the last time its quirks – a squeaky floorboard here, a child's pencil-mark on the plaster there. Never did replace that cracked kitchen tile.

Instinctively, I touched every door handle and light switch – because Olive would have touched them at some time. Silly, yes, but emotion rules. Pull the front door latch. Good and hard. Hear it echo through the empty rooms. Don't look back. Keep walking. A chapter closed. A new one opens. Life in all its guises.

Sing! Sing! Sing!

GAY BYRNE IS TREATING US ON LYRIC FM TO two hours of the Benny Goodman *Live at Carnegie Hall* concert recorded in January 1938. Sheer bliss! If you are into swing music, then here is the king and this is the ultimate royal banquet! O to have been there! If we ever master time travel, this will be one of my stopping-off points. There is such *joie de vivre* in the whole performance. The music bounces along with such infection that it is easy to imagine bopping in the aisles to such Goodman classics as 'Don't Be That Way', 'And the Angels Sing' and 'Blue Skies'.

For now we must make do with the recording – now digitally mastered. Thank heaven someone had the foresight to record the concert. There is a story (which Gay refutes, but it is at the least a good story) that Goodman had it recorded on one solitary microphone – what a take! – but did not release it until eleven years later. Whether or which, it is great to have it on record, and seventy-three years later it's as fresh as ever. The world was on the brink of war and here comes the happiest of music from a band of true artists in New York. Thank God for music, for the genius of Benny Goodman and for the invention of recording.

Here comes 'Blue Room'. To the aisles! To the aisles!

Lir

I AM IN TULLYNALLY ESTATE, CO. WESTMEATH, compiling material for a documentary on trees. My guide is Thomas Pakenham, who has travelled the world in search of remarkable trees. Here on his own estate, he introduces me to his pride and joy, the Great Beech of Tullynally.

'I know this tree as an old friend and to take part in its life emotionally, I think it is important to name it. We call it King Lir – not the Shakespearean Lear, but the Irish Lir whose children were changed into swans by their wicked stepmother, Aoife, and sentenced to live forever on Lake Derravarragh, which is only a few miles from here. And isn't it regal? It was pollarded about two hundred years ago and five great trunks grew from the pollard point about twelve feet up. They arch up, fuse together and grow apart again. It's an extraordinary structure.

'Even though I know it so well, I'm always seeing different patterns in the changing light. Then there are seasonal changes as it goes in and out of leaf, and of course snow and frost make it a totally different experience. It's so full of life; I can hardly believe it is centuries old.

'But apart from its beauty and its architecture, this tree is a hugely complicated engineering structure. It holds together an enormous weight – maybe thirty tons of wood. It is an engine pumping water from the ground right to the top in the form of sap – a distance of some eighty feet. In order to stay alive, every single part of the tree has to be covered each year with fresh skin or bark. In those thirty tons of wood are miles of cabling which carries the sap. It's an amazing machine.'

We bow in deference and take our leave of King Lir.

Boghomage 1 – The Poet

I LOVE BOGLAND. I LOVE ITS WILDNESS, ITS openness, its darkness, its mystery, its loneliness, its scents, its colours, its silence. It is like a great altar for worship, reflection, healing. Although my childhood memory of the bog is speckled with the pain of an aching back, the scorching heat of an unrelenting sun, a misery of midges and the danger of a near-drowning in a boghole, I love to go back to the bog whenever I can – just to *be* there.

My fellow Meathman, the poet Francis Ledwidge, loved the bog and it was his memories of the bog and Boyne country that kept him sane as he soldiered through the madness of the trenches of the First World War. From there he wrote to a publisher friend …

> Just now a big strafe is worrying our dugout and putting out our candles, but my soul is by the Boyne cutting new meadows under a thousand wings and listening to the cuckoo at Crocknaharna.

And to his friend Lizzie Healy, he wrote in July 1917:

> It must be quite beautiful on the bog now. How happy you are to be living in peace and quietude where birds still sing and the country is wearing her confirmation dress. Out here the land is broken up by shells and the woods are like skeletons … Please, dear Lizzie, send me a flower from the bog, plucked specially for me. I may be home again soon. In fact, I am only waiting to be called home. God send it soon.

Nineteen days later, Ledwidge was indeed 'called home' – blown to pieces by a stray shell.

Boghomage 2 – The Artist

AS PART OF THE RADIO SERIES *This Place Speaks to Me*, I took the artist Paddy Graham back to a childhood scene – Monaghanstown Bog, near Mullingar. These were some of his reflections …

'I always had a great sense of religion about this place. I would sit here as a boy and have a primal experience of this deep, rich, luscious bogland … I would look up at the sky with the larks hanging there and then back down to earth in a great circular sweep. I understood nature and God like that for years.

'As a child, everything was at eye-level – the wonderful browns and purples, the flies and the midges hovering above. I could almost taste the sensuality of it all. This was the exotic – here in the heart of the Midlands. You didn't need to travel in search of it. And then there was the great silence – which isn't silence at all, of course. If you slow down and listen, you will hear that choir of noises, an orchestra of beautiful sounds – buzzing, chirping, flitting.

'The bog "earths" you. You belong to it and you know you're going back to it. It's your home. I live now near the sea in Dun Laoghaire, but the bog is my home. I love the "thatch" on top of it and the rich female sensual earth underneath.

'This is where I pray. I don't say words. I just look and listen. It's a prayer of wonder about nature.'

In Auschwitz

ITS VERY SOUND STRIKES COLD INTO YOU.
Auschwitz. It calls up images of unimaginable
suffering, unknowable brutality. The images
give way to the reality of a grey, misty
September morning in 2004 when our coach
rumbled into the huge car park and we joined
the seemingly endless queues to experience
Auschwitz. Just to walk through the brick
quarters of Auschwitz One is two hours
of heartbreak. The displays of mountains
of suitcases, of shoes, of women's hair, of
spectacles – there is no escaping the grim
reminders of how horrific this place was
sixty years ago. The punishment cells, the
standing-up cells, the execution courtyard,
the gas chamber, the incineration ovens, the
barbed wire. No words can describe this …
or Auschwitz Two (Birkenau) a few miles
away, even more terrifying in its now empty
vastness. The experience burns itself deep
into the sub-conscious, never to leave it.

That evening, I wrote …

I do not want to be here – but I am
I try not to remember – but I must
I want to leave this place – and I can
With my head full of
Cascades of hair
Mountains of suitcases
And shoes and shoes
And children's shoes.

They did not want to be here – but they were
They tried not to remember – but they did
They wanted to leave this place – but they
  failed
Leaving only
Cascades of hair
Mountains of suitcases
And shoes and shoes
And children's shoes …

JOHN QUINN

Father and Son

I HAVE BEEN READING WITH GREAT DELIGHT *The Home Place*, Brian Leyden's memoir of growing up in Arigna, Co. Leitrim. I love his easy direct style of writing. Sometimes a passage of his will take your breath away, not just for its style but for the warm, empathic chords it strikes. Here he recalls a beautiful education imparted by his father to the young Brian, beginning in an old railway carriage …

'One summer I began to hear a strange scratching sound. I couldn't place the noise until my father found the source: wasps chewing the timber sides of the wooden carriage with their strong mandibles to make paper for their nest. It enthralled me to hear my father use words like mandible, pulp and regurgitate …

'As I grew older he would explain the difference between onion sets and shallots and the distinction between hardy annuals and perennials. He gave me an additional language of antique garden weights and measures: the linear inch, foot and yard; the surveyor's link, pole, perch, chain and rod; the Troy grain and penny weight; the avoirdupois ounce, pound and hundredweight; the liquid gill, pint, quart and gallon. A beautiful, granary-rich language that perfectly fitted parcels of turned earth, palmfuls of dry seeds and wheat grains. And he spoke a further garden vocabulary too, as moist and yielding on the tongue as bruised fruit, words like tuber, tendril, succulent, legume and loam: supple and pleasing descriptions that harmonised with my feelings for the natural world.'

How truly blessed you were, Brian.

Funny You Should Say That

WHAT IS THE FUNNIEST SENTENCE YOU HAVE ever read? A difficult question. Humour is such a subjective thing – like beauty, it is in the eye of the beholder.

I am currently re-reading *The Catcher in the Rye* and there are undoubtedly a few gems in there. I always liked Spike Milligan's request that his epitaph be 'I told you I was ill'. But the sentence that really bowls me over turned up in a most unlikely place – in David McCullagh's excellent biography of John A. Costello, *The Reluctant Taoiseach*. Costello's father came from County Clare and he loved telling his family stories about that county, particularly about the famed West Clare Railway. Indeed he claimed a printed notice in one station outlined a revised timetable and ended with a warning that 'there will be no last train'.

Only in Ireland and especially only in West Clare could someone come up with a surreal statement like 'There will be no last train'. I laugh as I write those six words.

An Ordinary Wee Draper

HAD GORDON WILSON NOT LOST HIS LOVELY daughter Marie in the horrific Enniskillen bombing in 1987, he would have remained the 'ordinary wee draper from Enniskillen' that he claimed to be. He always denied that he was in any way 'special', but to me he was a man chosen for his time.

When he gave the *Open Mind* Guest Lecture in 1993, he simply told his story of Enniskillen. But his telling of it was so simple and so heartfelt that literally no one in the audience moved for minutes when it ended. And this is how it ended …

'The bottom line is love. I have used the word over thirty times tonight and I make no apology for doing so, because I cannot believe that the mind of man who can send men to the moon and bring them back, cannot find a solution for our lovely land with a little of the love of God in his heart. If I may quote from the Gospel of Saint Matthew, chapter 22:

Jesus replied: Love the Lord your God with all your heart and with all your soul and with all your mind. This is the first and greatest commandment. And the second is like it. Love your neighbour as yourself. All the law and the prophets hang on these two commandments.

So, if I accept those as the commandments of God – which I do – then I have to ask myself the question: 'Who is my neighbour?' And the answer I get is that my neighbour is not just the lady next door, and not just my Protestant neighbour, and not just my Catholic neighbour. Every man is my neighbour, and my neighbour must also include my terrorist neighbour, because Christ died for him too …

Keeping Going

I MET DARRAGH TODAY. ALTHOUGH HE IS A friend and neighbour, I had dreaded this meeting. A month ago, Darragh and Rebecca's two-year-old son Cian died in a tragic accident in the local crèche. The whole community's hearts went out to them. All we could offer was love, prayer and hope, but still it felt inadequate. And now here were the grieving couple on their first fragile foray into some kind of normal life – Rebecca in Galway and Darragh going about in his Jeep, 'doing a few things'. 'All we can do is keep going, day by day, for each other and for Jamie, Cian's little brother.' My heart broke for him all over again.

'People are so good,' Darragh continued. 'No one would take a penny – not the supermarket, not the pharmacist, not the people who made his little coffin, not the men who opened his granny's grave [she had died five months earlier] so that Cian could be with her again. People are so good. But nothing heals the pain – certainly not time. You just keep going. But he will never leave us. Only this morning when the sunlight came into the kitchen at a certain angle, I could see his handprints on the cooker …'

8.12.10

Another Text Message

DECEMBER 2010. MY SON DECLAN TEXTS ME. 'Interesting programme on Channel 4. Check it out!' I take his advice. The programme is *One Hundred Greatest Toys* as voted by Channel 4 viewers. As the programme unfolds, Declan is clearly reliving his childhood, texting me repeatedly as old favourites of his come up. We both wonder what will be number one on the list. We are both wrong but Declan's wife, Kelly, guesses correctly. It is Lego – an old-fashioned toy which beats all the modern sophisticated technological gizmos out of sight.

After the programme Declan sends me a final text. 'Do you remember me and you making that Lego helicopter that you got for me on my birthday? It was on the floor of the living room in the little house on the prairie one summer many moons ago. It took us about two hours!'

The 'little house on the prairie' was a holiday home in Rosslare. It was 'many moons ago' – at least a quarter of a century, when Declan was seven or eight.

You can build an awful lot more than a helicopter with Lego.

A Hive of Industry

ANOTHER DIP INTO THE 1937 SCHOOLS Folklore Collection. This time for a look at trades and crafts in my own native parish of Ballivor, Co. Meath. What an extraordinary range of specialised trades!

Michael Devine would make coops for your pigeons or baskets for your potatoes, while John Power specialised in *gobáns* – little baskets for a calf's head. Michael Sefton was a nailer, while McGuire from Longwood would make a sock for your plough. Burke's and Dixon's were two of a number of forges, Burke's specialising in making slanes for turfcutters. Mick Masterson, Thomas Kennedy and 'Jeanie the Heath' were among several besom (brush)-makers. The besom was made of heather tied with briar and was sold for a halfpenny at fairs.

Conor Bracken and Thomas Welton were fine hatters. The Keegans were weavers, as were the Raffertys, who acquired the nickname *Fídín* (*fíd* – tweed).

Andy Bligh was a dyer and 'Dan the Napper' came from Cavan to nap the flannel woven by the weavers. Quinn and Gibson were journeymen who made sieves (out of ash). There were a number of cobblers too, and Johnny Murray was reputedly the last shoemaker when he died in 1933. There were tinkers and coopers who could provide you anything from a noggin (drinking-vessel) to a keeve (a vat or tub). Halpenny was a thatcher and Pottertons had a grinding mill.

And when you came to the end of your days, the candlemaker supplied candles for your wake while you rested in a coffin made by Cusack of Longwood.

Yes of course these were distant harsh times and it's easy to grow nostalgic, but still, what industry there was within one parish!

The Dying Year

The year is dying in the night
Ring out, wild bells, and let him die.

Time to search out Tennyson's lines from 'In Memoriam'. This was never one of my favourite days. This year's demise is wrapped in a misty greyness which lends little cheer. Memories of absent ones drift through the mist.

Ring out the grief that saps the mind
For those that here we see no more

The newspapers are full of predictions for the year to come and the disappointments of this dying year. And there are many of the latter. Severe economic recession, a harsh winter, a banking system in near-ruin, natural disasters across the globe.

Ring out the want, the care, the sin
The faithless coldness of the times
…
Ring out old shapes of foul disease
Ring out the narrowing lust of gold.

Soon the partying will begin. Even though there is little to celebrate, we celebrate – with hope and trust for better things. A New Year is, as one writer said, our second birthday of each year. For me, this will be my seventieth New Year. A new decade. New dreams. In a short while I will honour my mother's custom of opening the front door to 'let the old year's bad luck out'. A New Year. We begin again.

The year is going, let him go
Ring out the false, ring in the true.

A Sixpenny Treasure

AS A BOOKLOVER, I FIND IT DIFFICULT TO resist the lure of secondhand bookshops and I particularly lament the passing of the bookstalls and bookbarrows which proliferated around Dublin some forty years ago – outside Greene's of Clare Street, along the Quays, outside Roches Stores. It was in one of those that I bought a sixpenny treasure all those years ago. One had to search through the dross – the *Racing Calendar* of 1927 or *Geography of the British Empire* – but invariably there was a nugget to be found among 'All books on this stall – price 6p'.

This particular treasure was *The English Language – Its Grammar, History and Literature*, by J. D. Meiklejohn, 466 pages, hardbound, twenty-ninth edition, published 1909. The author, then Professor of Education at St Andrew's University, had quite a sideline in the textbook market, for this book is but one in a lengthy series of textbooks in English, history, geography and maths penned by the good professor.

The English Language is an amazingly rich compendium of knowledge about the development of that language. In the etymology section I found the most splendid jewels in this treasury. A 'butler', was in charge of 'butts' or casks of wine; a little butt was a bottle. 'Humble-pie' was made of the 'umbles' or entrails of a deer. 'Bombast' originally meant cotton-wadding. 'Rhubarb' comes from *Rha barbarum*, the wild plant of the river Rha (Volga). 'Ster' was originally the feminine of 'er', the suffix for a male agent. Hence baker and baxter, weaver and webster. On and on it goes, endlessly fascinating. All this and grammar and a history of English literature too.

Thank you, Professor. Sixpence well spent.

Star

I HAVE ONLY ONCE EVER BEEN IN THE STAR's dressing room and not – I hasten to add – because I was the star! The occasion was an interview with Spike Milligan about his childhood, and the venue was the Number One dressing room in the Gaiety Theatre, Dublin, where he was performing his one-man show.

It was at times like this that I realised how privileged I was in my career to meet people of international standing from many disciplines – literature, theatre, education, etc. Here I was in the star's dressing room with one of my great idols – Spike Milligan, comic, writer, Goon. Here he was – warm, accommodating and searingly honest …

'When I was given responsibility, I couldn't cope. I let my wife down. I let my army colleagues down. I let everybody down.'

A troubled man. I could see the pain in his eyes. I wanted to hug him. He was marvellously evocative in his recollection of the sights, sounds and colours of the India of his childhood. While there were occasional sparkles of wit:

> My Uncle Hughie was a very good athlete – and a lunatic! He used to dress up as Tarzan and play the saxophone while flexing his muscles! –

it was, in the main, a serious and measured interview, so much so that when editing it in studio, the sound engineer doubted if it was Spike at all that was on tape. He was expecting the non-stop clown. Wait until the end, I advised him.

At the end of the interview I said – 'Spike Milligan, thank you very much.'

> Goon voice: 'Oh that will be a pound, if you please …'

Stone Walls

LIVING IN THE WEST OF IRELAND, STONE walls feature prominently in my landscape. They are obvious examples of the practical use of the environment – clearing the (many) rocks from the land and using these rocks to mark the boundaries of the fields. They are also works of art in their simple construction, with wonderful features such as stiles and *púiríns* (gaps to allow sheep to pass through). Simple in their construction yes, but simple to construct? Try it sometime!

I was forced to try when part of my garden wall collapsed. I re-assembled the wall quite quickly and was feeling proud of my handiwork – until I barely leaned on it. The whole section came crashing down again. Beginner's ill-luck, I thought, but my second attempt proved equally disastrous. I gingerly made a third reconstruction. Visually it looked fine but I knew if I breathed heavily on it …

Confused, I sought a neighbour's advice. He took a long studied look at my effort. 'The secret,' he said eventually, 'is what you do with the small stones.' He proceeded to undo my work (easily done) and rebuild it, cleverly using the small stones as wedges and holding pieces. 'The small lads are the boys that hold everything together,' he said, seating himself comfortably on the repaired wall.

There's a large moral in that little experience.

Forbidden Fruit

ONE OF THE GREAT CRIMES OF MY childhood was to steal a toy truck from Michael Leddy's shop in Ballivor, Co. Meath. I derived no great joy from it, as I had to keep it hidden – but at least I was never found out. Unlike Gay Byrne, who related his sad tale to me for the book *Must Try Harder*:

'I am in High Babies in Rialto National School eating a juicy red apple which I have nicked from Monaghan's Corner Shop that morning. The teacher fingers me and that afternoon squeals on me to my mother about eating an apple in class. She knows I had no money to buy the apple and therefore I must have nicked it. She marches me home, orders me to produce my moneybox – which probably had about nine old pence in it –

and marches me back to Monaghan's shop.

'The shop is crowded (in my estimation about two million people are there) and in the loudest possible voice she announces to all and sundry (i.e. the two million in the shop and another four million passing by) what I have done and that I am here to make restitution, as the catechism used to say. Handing the moneybox to Mr Monaghan, she demands that he take the price of the apple therefrom. He produces a vicious-looking bacon knife, and after much manoeuvering and downright butchering of the little red moneybox I had got from Santa, he manages to prise out two pence – the price of the apple.

'My shame is complete when Mammy orders me to apologise for my evil deed to all present (at this stage, at least fourteen million). Somehow I force the words out. There is silence. I am a broken man. Well, a broken High Baby, at least …'

Finding a Balance

IT IS 1999. I AM ATTENDING A MAJOR conference in Ennis on the theme of 'Finding a Balance in Life'. One of the speakers is Ger Loughnane, former Clare hurler and team manager. I interview him at a very late hour. The following are some of his observations …

'The greatest thing sport has taught me is the importance of family. There is nothing like the thrill of meeting your family after winning – or their understanding when you have lost. They know more than anyone what you have gone through. The trick is to find the balance between not being over-euphoric in victory (leading to complacency) and not being too down in defeat. As the boxer said – it's not about being knocked down, it's about getting up again. Balance is really the secret of happiness in life. We can never achieve it completely but we can always aim closer. It's about savouring the everyday things – waking up beside your wife, chatting to the kids over breakfast, walking the dog, meeting the neighbours for a chat. My father bequeathed me a small farm in east Clare and my greatest thrill is to walk those fields at the weekend. It literally keeps me earthed.

'I am reminded of the great Olympic swimmer Matt Biondi. At the 1988 Olympics he won five gold medals and *only* came second in the sixth event (which would be a huge achievement for any athlete). The media descended on him and suggested he must be devastated to miss out on a sixth gold medal. 'Yeah, I'm a bit disappointed,' he replied. 'I gave it my best shot. But look, when I go home, my dog will still lick my face …'

'Sport is serious. You prepare very hard. You sacrifice a lot. But, regardless of the result, when you go home, the dog will still lick your face.'

Heroes

THEY SAY YOU SHOULD NEVER MEET YOUR heroes, rather hold their image at a distance, unspoiled. I don't agree. While I never met Ray Conniff physically, I spoke with him on the telephone and corresponded with him by letter. Those 'meetings' only enhanced my image of him.

Ray Conniff was, for half a century, a musician, arranger and bandleader whose distinctive sound – particularly his use of a wordless chorus – entertained millions of people worldwide. The second LP I ever bought (secondhand!) was his *Broadway in Rhythm*. It is playing as I write and is still fresh and vibrant fifty years after I purchased it in Caroline Records in Dublin. In gratitude to Ray for all the pleasure his music had afforded me over the years, I made a radio documentary in the form of a fan letter to him (*Dear Ray Conniff*) and duly sent a copy to his Los Angeles home. This gave rise to the phone-calls and correspondence. He was a very pleasant and modest man, now in his eighties, and was thrilled to be recognised by the documentary.

In 2001, my wife Olive died suddenly and when I sent birthday greetings to Ray later that year I told him his music had been a great comfort in my loss. To my utter delight I received a handwritten letter from the great man a couple of weeks later. It ended:

> Please accept my condolences on the loss of your wife. 'In all thy ways acknowledge Him and He will direct thy path …' Perhaps these words from the Bible will help fill the void.
> Kind regards,
> Ray

Ray himself died a year later. I hope he knows how much higher than ever he rates on my heroic scale.

In Highgate Cemetery

I LOVE VISITING CEMETERIES. THERE IS nothing ghoulish about this. Cemeteries are havens of peace and tranquility at the outset but they are places of intrigue also. Here are stories. Here are lives. Here is history.

My daughter lives in the Highgate district of London, and when I visit her, I invariably pay a visit to the wonderful Highgate Cemetery. Opened a century and a half ago, it is still a working cemetery despite having closed in 1975 when it was deemed to be commercially unviable. Many of the older graves are almost inaccessible, lost in a tangle of trees, ivy, ferns and mosses. This adds to the place's mystery, but despite its almost jungle-like appearance in spots, there is now a policy of 'managed neglect' which attempts to balance the cemetery's important ecology with its primary purpose as a resting place for the departed.

Easily the most visited 'resident' in Highgate is Karl Marx. Fewer than a dozen attended his funeral in 1883 but as his influence grew, so did the number of visitors seeking his grave. A massive bust of Marx sits atop his memorial which bears the inscription:

> The philosophers have only interpreted the world in various ways. The point is to change it.

For the visitor to Highgate, there is history down every walkway. Here lies Mary Ann Evans, better known as the great novelist George Eliot. And William Alfred Foyle, who began selling secondhand books in 1903 and went on to create 'the greatest bookshop in the world'. Across the way from him lies Douglas Adams. I wonder what part of the galaxy he has reached with his *Hitchhiker's Guide*. Further down we meet the great

Australian artist, Sidney Nolan. Over by the roadside is the tomb of William Friese-Greene, whose claim is to have been the 'inventor of kinematography'. That prince of the stage, Sir Ralph Richardson, is a near neighbour to Sandy Wilson, architect – designer of the magnificent British Library. Frank Matcham, who designed and built many of London's great theatres such as the Coliseum and the Palladium, is here, as are entertainers and musicians like Leslie Hutchinson, Max Wall, Shura Cherkassky.

I could spend hours in company like this but the visitors' bell is ringing. 'If you want to stay longer, it would cost you …' the girl in the ticket office jokes.

On the way out I notice the memorial (huge marble tomes) of a recent 'resident', Jeremy Beadle – 'Writer, Presenter, Orator of Oddities. Ask My Friends!' Making my way though an overgrown section, I am reminded of Shakespeare's words:

Golden lads and lasses must
As chimney-sweepers come to dust

Seen and Not Heard

I NEVER CEASE TO MARVEL AT THE ENERGY of young children. They seem programmed to be in a constant state of motion – running, jumping, falling, creeping, weaving, climbing. Pausing for rest or reflection and then off again. What a culture shock it must be for them to attend school for the first time. A barrage of commands greets them. Stand! Sit! Don't talk! Walk – don't run! I am aware that nowadays the infant classroom is a place of relative freedom, but I have been in schools where old ways die hard …

Such schools remind me of our son Declan's experience of the infant classroom. He had previously enjoyed the fun and freedom of Mrs Griffin's playschool, literally next door to his own home. But 'school' was different – distant from home, with large classes – and much more regimented. His first teacher was an ageing nun who clearly harked back to the 'seen and not heard' days of her own childhood. By the end of the first week, Declan was not a happy boy. 'It's not fair,' he sighed. 'You have to stand up straight with your hands by your side – and you're not even allowed to *whistoper* …'

A friend recently told me of a similar experience. Little boy goes off to school. Doting mother anxiously enquires each day what he has learned. No reply for the first week. Mother persists. Finally he cracks, 'All I know is you have to sit in the f -----g *cathaoir* all the time.'

You could say he was acquiring a proficiency in languages.

Entombed

ONE OF MANY PRIVILEGED MOMENTS I experienced as a radio producer was to gain entry to a five-thousand-year-old passage tomb in Knowth, Co. Meath. It is June 1995. I am making a programme in the series *The Mark of Man* in the distinguished company of archaeologist Frank Mitchell and historian George Cunningham. The passage tombs of Knowth and Newgrange are structures of marvel and mystery. Who built them? Who was buried here? Why here? We still don't know. 'We're not talking about a heap of stones thrown together,' says Frank. 'Those Stone Age settlers would have had the equivalent of modern quantity surveyors and architects. Those quartz stones would have come from Wicklow and those granite ones from the Mournes. An amazing achievement ...'

The central mound at Knowth was only excavated by George Eogan just over fifty years ago. Frank Mitchell worked on that excavation. He recalls the first time he entered the tomb. 'The Stone Age people had lit a lot of fires in there. The walls were covered in soot. What astounded me was that later Christian settlers had drawn figures in the soot. We could still make out their doodles.'

There are seventeen smaller satellite mounds around the central mound. To my delight, we are allowed enter one of them. We squirm and worm our way down the passage. It is an extraordinary privilege to stand at the end of this five-thousand-year-old structure and wonder at its purpose and its construction. 'You are standing just where cremated remains were deposited,' Frank reminds me. I fall silent in prayer and in memory.

Two Ladies

'TWO LADIES OF GALWAY' WAS HOW GEORGE Bernard Shaw described them in a poem he wrote to them as children. They are Anne and Catherine Gregory, granddaughters of Lady Gregory of Coole Park. They are in their eighties now and they have come back to Coole at my invitation to make a radio documentary about their extraordinary childhood there. Anne has written a delightful book, *Me and Nu*, about that childhood. In that book, she recalls how the Irish-American lawyer John Quinn – a close friend of Lady Gregory – used send them a case of apples every Christmas. It seemed entirely fitting therefore that this latter-day John Quinn should present a bag of apples (from the fruit and veg shop in Gort) to these charming ladies on first meeting them … They are suitably impressed.

We spend a wonderful two days revisiting scenes of their childhood in Coole, the Burren and Galway. They have brilliant memories of the luminaries who came to visit their grandmama – Yeats, Shaw, O'Casey, Synge. They had an idyllic childhood – they recall with glee how they would spend the entire day exploring the woods of Coole. They needed food of course, so they would fill up the legs of their knee-length knickers with apples … They giggle at the memory of the day when, thus encumbered, they met their mother and the artist Augustus John. Mother was disgusted and insisted they empty their knickers there and then. The shame of it, in front of Mr John – who was helpless with laughter …

Before we part. I ask Anne to sign my copy of her book, which she does, graciously.

Thank you John Quinn (Mark 2) for the apples. Sadly, we could not carry them as in our childhood.

Broadcasting Debut

ANOTHER FIRST. THE FIRST INTERVIEW I ever recorded for broadcasting on national radio. The year was 1979. It had been designated International Year of the Child. I proposed a series called *I Remember, I Remember*, in which guests would recall their childhood memories and influences. The pilot programme would feature Seán McBride, lawyer, politician and human rights activist.

It was a nervous *debutante* who invited Mr McBride to the radio studio, but he was most courteous and co-operative. His beguiling French accent added colour to the interview. As the son of Maud Gonne and Major John McBride – both heavily involved in the republican movement (his father was executed in 1916) – his was no ordinary childhood. Much of it was spent in France where he met a number of Irish literary figures. He had wonderful memories of flying kites on a Normandy beach with William Butler Yeats ('He was much better at the kites than me'). His favourite was the writer James Stephens, who would help him indulge in his hobby of stamp collecting and then treat him to ice cream and cakes in a Parisian *pâtisserie* – and enthrall the young boy with a fund of stories.

The pilot was deemed successful and the series went ahead. I was off on a new and enriching career. I could get to enjoy this – and did for the next twenty-five years.

A Week of Moments

SOMETIMES IT IS ONLY IN RETROSPECT THAT the import and impact of particular moments strike you. That was certainly the case in a memorable week in August 1965. It was the final week of a five-week study tour of American Education by a group of Irish teachers, of which I was fortunate to be a member.

Monday 16 August: In Gettysburg for a most atmospheric tour of the historic battlefield. Then a wonderful surprise, thanks to our leader, Stephen Daly. He managed to get us an audience with local resident, former president Dwight Eisenhower. He had already turned down ten requests that day, so we slipped in the back door! We had a friendly chat with this most congenial man for twenty minutes. A moment to treasure!

Tuesday 17 August: Washington DC. A reception for us in the Capitol office of Congressman John Fogarty. Mixing with a constant stream of congressmen when in walks Bobby Kennedy, who greeted us all individually. A very cool and shrewd character who I thought looked tired, even old for his years. We sang 'The Boys of Wexford' for him before he left. Twenty minutes later in walks brother Ted, full of beans. 'Are there any schoolteachers here?' he enquires. Totally different to Bobby. Jolly and jovial, he burst into song with 'Kevin Barry' and followed it with 'Sweet Adeline.' Later that evening we went to the Watergate for an open-air concert featuring live cannons for the *1812 Overture.* What a night!

Wednesday 18 August: A very moving visit to Arlington Cemetery to the grave of a fallen leader.

Thursday 19 August: An enjoyable visit to Goddard Space Centre is cut short as we are to meet President Johnson in the Oval Office! Shook hands with each of us. A very genial type who joked about the Irish running his life in Washington. We had a wonderful twenty minutes in the White House.

Lazy Days

ROBYN ROWLAND IS AN IRISH-AUSTRALIAN poet who spends part of her year in Connemara. She visits our village, Clarinbridge, regularly, for readings and workshops. I like her work. It is vibrant and sensuous. I particularly like this poem, 'Snapshot'. It was written a week after the 9/11 attacks on the United States. In the midst of our hurried and chaotic lives, we all need a 'lazy day' now and then.

SNAPSHOT

Dandelions drowse in the heat:
September, and summer still lingers.
Spangles of bright gorse dawdle up the bog
*   hills*
into the grey rock of a ruin opposite the house.
Connemara basks, open and safe,
our finger of peninsula barely lapped
by a placid sea.
Stillness swallows bird song.
Out on the strand at Omey Island

we hunt razor fish for our supper,
burrowing deep into the graveyard
of their cut-throat shaped shells
spiked upright in the sand.
Camouflaged with draped weed,
they ambush my unsuspecting step
that carries home the crescent moon
sliced into my foot.

Later, we gorge on them coated in garlic
and drink too much wine:
we need this lazy day,
this bandaged memory.

Katie

ANOTHER PHOTOGRAPH WHICH HAS survived a few generations and somehow come into my possession. It was taken in 1936 when cameras were still a novelty. Two women are standing in a potato field in County Monaghan. It is a very dark photo, not helped by the black attire worn by both women. It could easily have come from the Victorian era. The older woman is my paternal grandmother. It is the only photograph I have seen of any of my grandparents. She looks austere, but that again may be because of the 'widow's weeds' she is wearing.

The other woman is her only daughter, my aunt Katie. She faces the camera shyly. This is possibly a new, if not a first, experience for her. She is about thirty years of age. I can read uncertainty in her face. She has had a hard life so far and it won't get much easier. Taken out of primary school to help at home, her father deceased, her mother aged, she now shares a home with three of her five brothers, all single. What if one of them were to marry? It would be difficult for Katie to stay on, especially when her mother passed on. Katie eventually married late and had a difficult life.

I loved Katie. She was warm and giving and accepted her lot in life with quiet resignation. When I wrote my novel *Generations of the Moon*, I dedicated it to Katie and based the character of the heroine Bridie on her. I did it as a tribute to a kindly woman and to many women like her who made major sacrifices for their families. She would of course be highly embarrassed. 'Och now,' she would sigh gently, 'there was no call for you …' There was every call, Katie. There was every call.

My Education

YOU WILL NEVER FIND THE NAMES BILL Kelly, Colm Murtagh or Harry Garry in a textbook of great educators – except in the book of my education. They were all characters from my childhood, each of whom contributed to my development.

Bill Kelly was a blacksmith. To witness him practise his dark arts amid steam and smoke in the village forge was an education in itself, but the real learning came on his daily visit to our kitchen for his dinner. The meal was followed by a compulsory game of draughts, when the self-proclaimed 'king of the board' would challenge me to 'a crack at the title'. Bill taught me about losing and (eventually) winning and he made me laugh. Colm Murtagh was the local curate. He brought us altar-boys on annual outings. I remember in particular my first experience of a musical show when we went to see Romberg's *New Moon* in Trim. It was a wonderful introduction to the world of theatre and music. And Harry Garry was the shopkeeper in the local grocery store who greeted me unfailingly with a smile and a joke. I was important even if I only came in search of a penny toffee.

All of them had time for me and had an interest in my life. It takes a village to raise a child.

Tacit Knowledge

I LOVED JOHNNY KELLY. HE WAS A BOGMAN, in the literal sense of that word. Born, reared and lived all his life in a simple tin-roofed cottage in the bog near where I grew up in County Meath. But to me he was the wisest of men. He knew the lore of the bog - its history and stories. He knew the quality of turf mined from that bog. He could tell who made the slane for cutting turf – 'I'd say by the look of it, it's a Burke!' His speech was rich in idiom – 'I was so hungry, I could eat the sock of a plough!' He knew his own place and would wish for no other.

Johnny never went beyond primary school, but his knowledge surpassed that of many who had strings of qualifications to their names. It was a tacit knowledge – an acquisition of things we know but cannot tell. We acquire them through working with materials, through practice with others, through absorption. The man who has 'a good eye for a horse' never developed that eye from studying textbooks. Since that knowledge cannot always be written down or stated explicitly, our system of education often ignores it. Linguistic ability is valued more than real intelligence.

Johnny could never produce an essay on bogland flora and fauna, or write the handbook on turfcutting, but he knew all about *cíob* and *spadach*, how to make a *scup* to drain a boghole, and how to wield a slane with complete dexterity. That, for Johnny, was 'the real ass's milk!'

The Beauty of Water

I LIVE IN CLARINBRIDGE, A VILLAGE IN south Galway. Clarinbridge. The bridge over the river Clarin. The bridge is beautiful – stone-cut with three arches. The river is equally beautiful, but then so are all rivers. Its moods reflect the seasons. It can be angry, zesty, playful, placid, sullen. Water is such an amazing resource. It is life for our planet. Its sight and its sound alone can cheer us, comfort us, heal us. And yet we take it so much for granted. It will not always be so, as clean water becomes more and more a precious resource. It is said that water will be the new oil in the future. Wars will be fought over it. It need not happen of course – if only we cherish it, care for it, respect it.

I love to stand on that bridge and watch the water's movement, ponder its mystery, give thanks for its presence in our lives. Each time I cross the bridge – which is a few times each day – this reflection comes to me unbidden …

We thank you Lord for the gift of water,
for its life, its energy, its constancy,
for its light and its shade
for its song and its dance
for its flow and its counterflow.
May all the waters of the earth give you praise
and may we be forgiven
for the way we have abused, polluted and
  wasted your gift.
In your mercy, look down on those
who suffer from a surfeit or a scarcity of water
across the world.

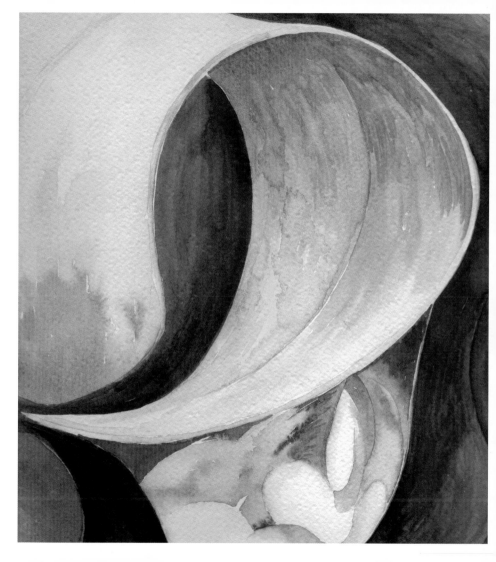

Fear

JOHN O'DONOHUE OFTEN RELATED THE classic 'fear' story from India.

A man is condemned to spend a night in a cell with a poisonous snake. If he moves, the snake will attack and kill him. So he spends the night standing in a corner, frozen with fear, eyeing the coiled deadly threat in the opposite corner. The night wears on. The man desperately fights off sleep and is relieved to welcome the dawn. The snake never moves. When the full light of day comes into the cell, the 'snake' is revealed as an innocuous coil of rope.

Fear insinuates itself so much into our lives – fear of the unknown, of failure, of being ourselves, of illness, of death. And yet so often it turns out to be a pile of old rope that petrifies us. Groundless fears that immobilise us. We waste the night waiting for the dawn. What we have to do, says John O'Donohue, is to face up to our fear and name it. When we do that, the fear begins to shrink. 'What am I afraid of?' is a very liberating question, John suggests. Easier said than done, but he reminds us that there is lots of encouragement in the Bible. According to John, the phrase 'Be not afraid' occurs 366 times in the Good Book – 'one for every day of the year,' John laughs, 'and one for luck!'

Made to Measure

WE ARE CONSTANTLY REMINDED THAT WE live in a knowledge-based society, but too often knowledge is equated with information and it is (wrongly) assumed that everything that is worth knowing can be measured. Nowhere is this more glaringly evident than in our public examination system. Grades and points are the ultimate goal for all second-level students. The Leaving Certificate becomes the 'Points Race' which will decide entry to the third-level system – and the media feed on that.

A fine example of this was a feature some years ago in a national newspaper on 'the 600-point girl' – a student who had secured the magical maximum points for college entry the previous year. Almost an entire page was devoted to 'how she did it'. She did it by 'learning the formula for each exam and practising it endlessly … I knew exactly what was required in each question … I learned off the sample answers provided by the examiners … I was always frustrated by teachers who would say – "You don't need to know this for the exams, but I'll tell you anyway"…'

I compliment the girl. She played the system and won. I accuse the system. I am mindful of the words of a wise genius, Albert Einstein:

> Not everything that is countable counts and not everything that counts is countable.

If I had the power, I would have those words carved in stone over the entrance to every school in the country.

Questioning George

AS THE SONG HAS IT, 'SOME DAYS ARE diamond, some days are stone'. Among the diamond days of my broadcasting career, the recording of the 1998 Open Mind Guest Lecture in University College Cork would be in the very top rank. The speaker was Senator George Mitchell, who had earlier that year facilitated the Good Friday Agreement in Northern Ireland. I was so honoured and privileged that he agreed to give the Open Mind Lecture. It took place in Cork because he was being honoured by the city's university. He gave a wonderful presentation on the future of Northern Ireland and then said he would take questions from the floor. We kept the tape rolling, hoping for maybe another ten minutes ….

It was while we waited for the first question that he totally disarmed us … 'I spent fifteen years in the United States Senate, where there is an unlimited right to debate. Any senator may speak at any time on any subject at any length, even though it has no relationship to the legislation being considered. So as Senate Majority Leader, I listened to sixteen-hour speeches, eleven-hour speeches. I didn't realise it at that time that the Lord, in the mysterious way in which he works, was preparing me for the negotiations on Northern Ireland! So I am quite prepared to speak for the rest of the night! One of the dubious skills I acquired in the Senate was the ability to speak at indefinite length, on any subject, with no notice, usually neither possessing nor conveying information!'

We were off! There followed another fifty minutes of insights and experience from this extraordinary man. We now had a second bonus programme, 'An Evening with George Mitchell.' Diamond.

The Kitchen

IT IS JUNE 2009. I STAND BEFORE THE LOCKED front door of a house. It is the house I was born in and in which I spent the first thirteen years of my life. It is now derelict – gaping holes in the roof, crumbling floors, broken windows. I have not set foot in this house for fifty-four years but now I am about to do so – with a film camera trained on my every move and reaction, for I am participating in a television documentary on my childhood. The producer whispers 'Go!' I take a breath and enter. I turn left automatically and find myself in the kitchen.

The house has not been inhabited for over a decade and the last tenants have left the place in a mess – broken furniture, discarded utensils and crockery, ankle-deep detritus. This is very difficult. I am expected to give a commentary as I scan the hearth of my childhood, with the camera hovering before me. The temptation is to cry 'Halt!', but the scene dissolves before me.

There is the range, Zebo-polished, with warmth radiating from it to the three figures seated before it – my mother, Kitty Carey and Katty Brown from down the village. Clink of teacups, aroma of soda bread, laughter and animated chatter. On a wall shelf, the radio emits *céilí* music. Seated at the kitchen table a boy wrestles with homework – simple interest sums, an English composition. He casts an eye at the press under the stairs. According to his brother who had a vivid dream, a pink horse resides in there. The sunshine sparkles on the window. Tibs the cat is curled under the range. The Sacred Heart smiles down on all from the opposite wall.

All is well. This is easy.

Bees

IF I TELL YOU THAT THE LAST RADIO documentary I made was entitled *The Singing Masons of Skehanagh*, you might well be puzzled as to what it was about. I borrowed half the title from Shakespeare. In a marvellous speech in *Henry V*, he describes bees as 'the singing masons building roofs of gold'. And that was my subject – bees. I had long been fascinated by their work and their social order, and I needed someone to tell their story. I found him in P. J. Ruane, a quiet-spoken farmer from Skehanagh (hence the title) in east Galway. P. J. – like Johnny Kelly of the bog – abounds in tacit knowledge, wisdom acquired by doing and observing, rather than by learning from books or college courses.

From the day forty-five years ago when, out of curiosity, he brought home a swarm of bees in a shoebox and housed them in a tea chest, P. J. has observed and learned from bees, arriving at the point where he and his late brother Tim were producing award-winning honey. He sits in his kitchen, sharing his wisdom with me. He still marvels at the social order of bees – from the 'superwoman' queen through the workers (who rotate their jobs of foraging, guarding, cleaning) to the lazy drones.

'Everyone should keep a hive. You learn so much about nature, hard work and social harmony. In her short six-week life, the worker achieves as much as a human does in fourscore years … They can travel up to ten miles in search of nectar, and when they find a good source, they do a figure-of-eight dance to alert others … They are so patient. They don't complain but just get on and do what has to be done. Humans could learn so much from them.'

I sat at the master's feet for an hour. 'Now, we'll have the tea,' declares P. J.

All this wisdom and ham sandwiches too.

Infinity

A NEWSPAPER REPORT INFORMS ME THAT astronomers scanning for objects at the very edge of the visible universe have discovered the earliest galaxy yet found. They believe it formed '*just* [my emphasis] 480 million years after the Big Bang that created space-time'. This makes the galaxy the most distant object to us that has been discovered to date. The astronomers reckon it is 'about 13.2 billion light years away ...'

How does one even begin to grapple with concepts like that? Reading the report took me back to a sombre day in September 2001. The world was still reeling from the Twin Towers horror of 11 September. Five days later I was in West Sussex in England recording an interview with the great astronomer Sir Patrick Moore. It was a World Day of Mourning for America's lost ones. At 11 a.m. there would be a silence observed. I thought it appropriate to stand in Patrick's garden, alongside his observatory. I looked at the brilliant clear sky out of which death had come in New York and remembered those who had died. I further reflected on how infinitesimal this planet is in the grand scheme of things and how much unnecessary hatred and futility there is on it ...

In truth, what do we know? Very little. The limits of our knowledge only stretch 'about 13.2 billion light years'.

And after that ...?

Hope

MID-JANUARY 2011. IT HAS BEEN A HARD winter. And a long one. Snow in November and freezing temperatures all through December. Record 'lows'. Who would have thought we would read of -18°C in Ireland? Travel disruption. And then the inevitable aftermath. Burst pipes, flooding, ruined roads. A hard winter – and of course it's not over yet.

But this evening two things give the heart a lift. Coming back from my afternoon walk (New Year resolution!) I notice a definite lengthening in the daylight. The sun hangs over Galway Bay at 5 o'clock, seeming almost unwilling to leave us. 'The cock's step on the manure heap is lengthening' was how my mother interpreted this phenomenon.

And in the sun's dying rays I catch sight of change in my little weeping willow in the front garden. A couple of weeks ago it was petrified in ice and snow. Now along its drooping branches tiny buds have appeared, tiny but firm and resolute. What a heart-warming sight! New life. Hope. Promise of warmer, greener days. Praise to the bud.

There's a lengthening in my own step now.

A Letter to the Editor 3

Stradbally North
Clarinbridge

19 August 2009

The Editor
The Irish Times
Dublin 2

Dear Madam,

Rosalie Pickering's recent question (Is Puck Fair? 12 August) suggested to me that there are many pressing topics that need to be addressed.

Is Achill Sound? Does Skellig Rock? Is Claregalway? Other topics that demand attention might include: Is Trim tidy? Is Birr cold? Is Bray within an ass's roar? Is Tipp top? (they might Kilkenny). We need to know.

Yours etc.
John Quinn

Peas in Our Time

IF THERE WAS EVER A COMPETITION FOR THE Most Boring Occupation on a Summer Afternoon in the Whole World EVER, shelling peas would surely be a strong contender. These were my thoughts on a sunny August afternoon as I seated myself at the patio table, my pea harvest in a bucket to my left and two empty pots – one for peas, one for pods – before me. Hopefully a mug of tea and a biscuit or two with some soothing background music on Lyric FM will help, but still … boring.

Maybe not, though. Once you get into a rhythm, learn how to split the pod with the thumb and tumble out the occupants, it's not too bad really. You play childish games. Quinn claims a world record with ten peas in a pod! Modestly acknowledges acclaim. Occasionally a brave if foolish pea leaps beyond the pot for freedom. I give a crazed cackle and in my best Colditz accent, announce that *All escapees vill be punished mit instant death*, i.e. they will be

eaten *now*. Mmm. They are so succulent. Late Flash! Quinn sets new record with ELEVEN! Now for the Magic Dozen, he says!

They are things of beauty. Peas. Nestling comfortably in their sealed pod. The miracle of nature. Only a few months ago I had gently pushed mother pea into the soil with my finger. And now this bountiful harvest on an August afternoon. The pods can be deceptive too. What seems bursting with promise can often be hollow inside. A bit like humans? Finished! Now for the freezer bags and the promise of homegrown produce for the winter.

Praise the Lord for peas!

JOHN QUINN

Early Reading

THE WORLD READING CONGRESS WAS HELD in Dublin in 1982. Hundreds of delegates from all over the world assembled to analyse and discuss the latest research on all aspects of reading. A special parents' session was held at St Patrick's College, Dublin. A thronged auditorium listened to the impassioned plea of Patricia Koppman for the involvement of children with books at the very earliest age. Patricia was the daughter of a preacher from the Deep South of the USA and her evangelistic zeal was having an effect on her audience.

Question time. A young mother tentatively raises a hand. 'At what age should I start reading to my child?' she asks. Patricia looks her straight in the eye. 'Well, honey,' she drawls, 'I'll spare you the delivery room … but on the way back to the ward, you could make a start.'

Laughter all round, but Patricia was deadly serious. You cannot start early enough to let the child experience books – hold them, chew them, play with them in the bath, watch and listen as the parent unravels their mystery until finally the child learns that by turning a page a new scene unfolds. And then another. And another, until in the end we have the magic of a story.

She didn't say as much, but I knew Patricia was implying that if the delivery was straightforward enough, why not welcome the child into the world with a story …

Teenager

JANIS IAN'S BEAUTIFUL SONG 'AT SEVENTEEN' is a poignant evocation of the awkward and difficult teenage years from a girl's point of view. It was, in my opinion, no easier for boys. I cringe at the memory of shyness, awkwardness, lack of self-esteem. The late Dermot Morgan knew about these things too. In his submission to the book, *Must Try Harder*, he recalled for me his desperate attempts at establishing himself as a 'hard man'.

'The "hard men" worked extremely hard at affecting their strut. John Wayne was their gait-way to the world. Obsessive gum-chewing and a technical mastery of the comb were other signals to an unsuspecting world. It was less grooming than preening. Nonetheless, a gum-chewing, hair-flicking man with a swagger was surely not to be taken lightly by the rest of the tribe. All those techniques however, were hopelessly insufficient if one hadn't studied that as-yet-unwritten but no-less-real work *One Hundred Cool Ways to Hold a Cigarette* …

'This then was the grand sight, the peacock in all his glory. It was with this reckless demonstration of bravado that the girls from Mount Anville or Foxrock were to have their heads turned and look in awe and wonderment. And doubtless they did turn their heads and did wonder, but not perhaps for the reasons he perceived …'

A Bilk Moment

ON *LYRIC FM* GAY BYRNE HAS JUST PLAYED A track by Acker Bilk. Music has such evocative power. I was immediately taken back to a June day in 1966. I was a patient in a TB sanatorium in Blanchardstown, Co. Dublin. Three months earlier I had met a very beautiful fellow-patient, Olive McKeever, and already I was in love with her. We utilised any excuse to be together – Sunday Mass, the Monday filmshow, afternoon walks, even bingo on Tuesday nights …

It was the feast of Corpus Christi and there would be a procession through the grounds. Another excuse to meet up! A PA system was strung throughout the procession route via the road lights. And then it rained on our parade. And it rained. And it rained. Mercilessly. Procession cancelled. Doom in the gloom. Mass was however broadcast from the hospital chapel over the PA system – and then a wonderful thing happened.

When Mass was over somebody linked BBC Radio to the PA system. And so, for a whole hour, *Ack's Back* – Acker Bilk and his music – echoed surreally through the sanatorium grounds. Through the ever-thickening mist I could see the unit wherein lay my beloved. I spent the afternoon writing another ten-page love letter which a nurse would hopefully smuggle into Unit Four. The plaintive clarinet of Acker Bilk wafting through the mist reflected my mood perfectly. Thank you, Acker.

Doing Nothing

Parent: Where were you?
Child: Out.
Parent: Where out?
Child: Out out!
Parent: What were you doing?
Child: Nothing.

There is, of course, no such thing as 'doing nothing'. No one has illustrated this better than the writer Seán Ó Faoláin in his autobiography, *Vive Moi!*, when he describes his annual escape from the poverty of Cork to his Auntie Nan's farm in County Limerick. There he did 'a blessed and glorious nothing' …

'I sat by a well and saw a spider race with delicate legs across the cold water from out of his cavern … I saw a line of cows pass along a road, their udders dripping into the dust … While all day Uncle Tom went slowly up and down the ridges on one knee thinning his turnips, I wandered. I saw a row of poplars whispering to the wind. I picked and chewed the seeds of the pink mallow. I saw how the branch of the thorn tree in the armpit of the alder had worn itself and its lover smooth from squeakingly rubbing against it for forty years. I saw an old ruined castle and a Big House with the iron gates hanging crookedly from its carved pillars …

'I lay on my back among lone fields and wondered whether the cloudy sky was moving or stopped … things from which a boy of this region would never get free, things wrapping cataracts of love about his eyes, knotting tendrils of love about his heart.'

What an education!

Life

TELEVISION OFFERS US SO MANY MOMENTS of wonder and awe. For me nothing surpasses the marvellous 2009 BBC series, *Life*. The wonders of the natural world are matched only by the wonders of technology as we are transported from the depths of the Arctic Ocean to the most arid stretches of African desert. With amazing cameras that can both slow down and speed up the fragile development of the tiniest plant or animal, the series reveals for us the extraordinary repertoire of survival strategies that the natural world has accumulated.

The capuchin monkeys raid the palm-nut tree for its ripest fruit. They tear the husk from a nut and leave it for a week to dry in the sun. Next they place it on a huge flat boulder which will be their anvil. Then with a large rock as their hammer, they smash the nut with persistence and dexterity.

Deep on the ocean floor, the recently mated octopus finds a large rock under which she can shelter. There she lays her eggs – all one hundred thousand of them. And there mother octopus will live for six months caring for and protecting her eggs, never leaving them until eventually she dies of starvation. Her ultimate sacrifice is rewarded as we watch the perfectly formed baby octopi emerge from the eggs.

The wise and measured commentary of the great David Attenborough guides us through the challenges of life, but the true heroes of this amazing series have to be the camera people who display endless patience and skill in the face of considerable risk and danger to bring those pictures into my living room. I salute them.

Salt and Pepper

TIM LEHANE HAS BEEN A VALUED FRIEND and colleague of mine since we both joined RTÉ Radio in the mid-1970s. Tim was a master-craftsman in the art of radio production, while I was more of a journeyman, but working in educational programmes, we both considered that we did important things. In the words of another radioman, Seán Mac Réamoinn, speaking of his pioneering days in outside broadcasts – *Rinneamar rudaí ab fhiú a dhéanamh* (We did things that were worth doing). Our programmes were broadcast to minority audiences at night. They would never have the mass appeal of the daytime chat shows.

'It's like this,' Tim argued one evening, while we were having tea in the canteen. 'Do you see the salt and pepper? That's us! We don't take up much space on the table, but we add spice to the meal!' I felt much better as we returned to the studio. The Spice Boys! That had a nice ring to it.

A Child's Gift

WE HAVE ALL BEEN RECIPIENTS. A CHILD presents us with a gift as a token of love or esteem. It may be the tackiest item in the pound shop or the most impractical item imaginable but because it was purchased with the child's mite or fashioned by the child's unsure hands, we treasure it for what it symbolises – love, innocence, generosity.

A former teaching colleague recalled for me an incident from early in his career. It was the mid-1960s and he had been teaching a class of fifty-five children in an inner-city Dublin school, 'lovely boys, never had a problem with them'. Now he was moving on. And on his last day in the school, the boys presented him with a gift package – a Child of Prague holy water font, a cigarette lighter and two boxes of matches! Naturally, he was very touched but he was puzzled by the boxes of matches. The boys' spokesman explained:

> Well, sir, we collected forty-nine pennies – one from everyone present today – and we went down to Hector Grey's at lunchtime. When we bought the holy water font and the cigarette lighter we had two pence left over. So we bought you the matches …

A love, an innocence, a generosity that would blow your heart open.

Below the Salt

A CHRISTMAS CARD FROM MIKE COOLEY brings an interesting enclosure. Mike is an engineer and a writer and broadcaster on work and technology. He is a great admirer of the craftspeople – 'unself-conscious artists' – he knew in his native, Tuam, Co. Galway, and he encloses a copy of his poem, 'A Grand Tour' – images of craft skills in 1940s Tuam. Here are a couple of verses …

A stone's roll downhill, almost unnoticed
hid the tiny snug leather-scented workshop of
*   shoemaker Doris Hosty.*
The shoe-last in the window –
a symbol and a tool with paraffin lamp of
*   eye-damaging inadequacy*
where handmade shoes seemed to grow from
*   the materials*
spread on a small work-surface
while throughout the town there was no
*   shortage of those to testify*
that the shoes she made would fit like a glove,

put a spring in your step and last for years.
One proud owner known for hyperbole
asserted that any self-respecting corpse
would be proud to be laid out in them.

Where to stop in this Hermitage of treasures?
*   Perhaps at Paddy Donoghue's*
whose hand stitched, brass embellished
*   harnesses set off many a fine horse,*
or famed footballer Frank son of Jim
*   Stockwell whose shop signs with letters*
defiantly stood proud of their flat surface.
Why not the bakers Clorans and Lydons
*   where ovens were fired up at around 4*
*   a.m.*
or Bob Holmes barber and provider of
*   apprenticeships?*
Not forgetting the Walsh brothers – a quartet
*   of tailoring talents*
three in Tuam and Richard in Kilcreevanty
or the Holian family of plasterers, bracklayers
*   and builders.*

Or Tommy Acton the bonesetter 'with the
gift' in Demesne cottages.

Now meandering along the Old Gardens
pathway
to the Old Road where the Rooney brothers
sculpted beneath the galvanised roof of their
windswept workspace.
There they 'liberated' Angels or Celtic Crosses
as if by magic
from the pregnant stone in which they could
already see the figure
and would remove 'all that was not David'
until he emerged resplendent.
Then the hand, eye and brain combined to
direct the spectacular chisel movements
and beneath its cutting edge, beauty was
manifest
Yet these artist craftspeople were kept 'below
the salt'
by the inadequate name – stonecutter.

Mike helpfully explains that in the Middle Ages, salt was placed mid-table. Those with title were above the salt, while commoners were 'below the salt'.

The Music of Words

AS A CHILD OF THE RADIO ERA, I REMEMBER being fascinated by the BBC Shipping Forecast – *Fastnet, Lundy, Sole, Plymouth* … In the confined Ireland of the 1950s they might well have been mysterious underwater kingdoms. The formal sonorous intonation of the announcer added to the intrigue but a part of the magic was in the very music of the names – *Portland, Wight, Dover, Finisterre* …

Children are naturally attracted to the music of words. Just eavesdrop on a child who picks up a strange place-name – *Abu Dhabi, Ballinabrackey* – and listen as they run and play with it. The children's writer Dorothy Edwards once told me a story that illustrates this perfectly. In the working-class area in which she grew up, a woman was about to give birth. The neighbouring women took over as was their wont, leaving the father-to-be at a loose end. 'Keep the other children busy,' he was told. 'Read to them or something.'

All went well. The child was safely delivered. The women relaxed with a pot of tea. Eventually they noticed that the children were very quiet. On investigation, they found the father sitting on the front doorstep reading to an audience of beguiled children. What was he reading? 'The only material he ever cared to read or possibly could read,' said Dorothy. 'The racing results from the evening paper!'

Rose of Troon, six to four on.
Doodlebug, twenty-five to one.
The Trickster, seven to two.

'Racehorses have such exotic or quirky or funny names. The music of those names was enough to sate his young audience …'

A Favourite Prayer

WE PRAY FOR MANY REASONS – THE overcoming of difficulties, the resolution of a problem, the easing of a worry. Seared into my memory is a prayer from over fifty years ago, when I was nervously approaching my Leaving Cert exam:

O great St Joseph of Cupertino, who by your prayers obtained from God that you be asked at your examination the only proposition you knew, obtain for me likewise …

My favourite prayer, however, comes from the pen of Cardinal John Henry Newman. He wrote learned treatises on topics theological and educational, but this simple prayer goes straight to the heart in its warmth and its reassurance. We all crave protection from life's buffeting and the knowledge that the Lord will be with us always and especially at the end of our days. Cardinal Newman captures this craving with his measured and affirming words.

May the Lord support us all the day long
Till the shadows lengthen
And evening comes
And the busy world is hushed
And the fever of life is over
And our work is done.
Then in His mercy
May He give us safe harbour
Peace at the end
And holy rest.
Amen.

Cramming

JOHN D. SHERIDAN WAS A HUMOROUS WRITER who wrote a weekly column in the *Irish Independent* in the 1950s and 1960s. The column featured his wry observations on everyday life. Burning issues such as 'The Right Time' and 'At the Barber's', and mundane topics such as 'Onions' and 'Hot Water Bottles' engaged his wisdom and wit.

He spent his latter days in a Dublin nursing home and it was there I encountered him to record for radio his memories of youth and of his teaching career. (I have to mention here that my conscience still assails me over his death. He died suddenly and was found slumped over his typewriter. He had been typing notes in anticipation of my visit … But then I console myself by reflecting that he died as he had lived, playing with words.)

On my first visit I could not help noticing the stack of prayer books and volumes of spiritual reflections neatly piled on top of his locker. He noticed my interest. 'Oh those,' he said dismissively, but with an impish grin. 'I'm just cramming for my finals!'

I have no doubt but that he got an honours first-class result.

On Being Brave

THE SPECIAL OLYMPIC WORLD SUMMER Games were staged in Dublin in 2003, during an unforgettable week of pride, pageantry and participation. The swimming competitions were held in the National Aquatic Centre.

In one heat of the 'Fifteen Metre Unassisted Swim' there are only three competitors. Each has an assistant following in the water, in case of emergency. A boy from the Seychelles wins the heat easily in 14.7 seconds. A boy from Honduras comes second in 17.97 seconds. All eyes turn to the third competitor. She is Hazel Zumbado, aged fifteen, from Costa Rica. She is deaf and mute and out of the water she is confined to a wheelchair, but she has the use of her arms and so can swim. She takes a long time to get going and the crowd responds to her huge effort.

Frank McNally catches the moment in his *Irish Times* report.

They are shouting, screaming, urging her every inch of the way; and her progress is measured in inches, as enormous effort translates into tiny advances through the water … There are now four assistants in the water, encouraging and ready to help if needed. But the swimmer is going to make it without their assistance, and with everyone in the packed gallery on his or her feet, applauding, she touches the wall in 1 minute 59.23 seconds.

How beautifully Hazel epitomised the Special Olympics motto:

Let me win, but if I cannot win, let me be brave in the attempt.

My Gardening Companion

WHETHER IN MY TURNING THE SOD IN spring or unearthing its fruits in winter, he seems to anticipate my arrival. There's a rustle in the hedgerow that seems to whisper – *You took your time! Thought you weren't coming!* Leaves flicker but I still can't detect him – until he flits down to within a metre of my spade and cheekily puffs out the fire-red brilliance of his chest. My heart lifts. I welcome him and hastily apologise for my tardiness. As if to punish me, he resumes his hide-and-seek game in the hedge. Now you see me, now you don't. The speed of his movement is amazing. He returns to the upturned soil. Standing there on his spindly legs, cocking an eye towards me as he pecks at the soil – he looks so fragile and so astoundingly beautiful.

We resume our conversation. Experts on the radio have convinced me that birds have memory, so I presume this is the same robin who cheered me last winter and who is therefore my special companion. My children used to tease me about talking to him but this is a true and important conversation. The poet John Clare would understand:

Sweet little bird in russet coat
The livery of the closing year!
I love thy lonely plaintive note,
And tiny whispering song to hear.
While on the stile, or garden seat,
I sit to watch the falling leaves,
The song thy little joys repeat,
My loneliness relieves.

Elsewhere

WHEN MAYO POET TERRY MCDONAGH GAVE a reading in our local tearooms, a line from one of his poems sang out to me –

I need an Elsewhere

It is so true. Amid the rough and tumble of life, enmeshed in fears and anxieties, buffeted by dangers and doubts, each of us needs an Elsewhere. A place to be alone, to be away from discord, to *be*. It may be – but does not have to be – a physical place. It just needs to be an Elsewhere. It set me thinking ...

A woodland walk
A singing stream
A fireside chair
To sit and dream.
   I need an Elsewhere ...

A storied ruin
An ancient tree

Lost in the swell
Of a great symphony
   I need an Elsewhere ...

A Kavanagh verse
A novel's lure
By waters wild
On a lonely moor
   I need an Elsewhere ...

A scent of leather
Children at play
A blackbird's song
As I turn the clay
   I need an Elsewhere.

Meandering

I LOVE THE WORD *meander*. ITS VERY SOUND rolls musically off the tongue. Meander. It depicts a mazy, sinuous movement, winding and weaving, pausing and moving on. Like a river. And of course that is the origin of the word. Meander is the name of a river in Asia Minor.

Penelope Leach loves the word too. Penelope writes on child development and in an interview with me she bemoaned the fact that children today are denied the opportunity to *meander* – the chance to pause and reflect, to stand and stare, to work things out. Instead, she claimed, because we are terrified that our children might be *bored*, we hurry them through their young lives, often organising their lives almost out of existence.

If this is Tuesday, it must be dancing lessons …

I was reminded of a time many years ago when I had youthful energy and enthusiasm. I did a study of children's leisure pursuits –

a major nationwide study. A friend in the research business persuaded me to use the diary method – give the children mini-diaries, blocked out in half-hours, in which they would record how they spent their leisure time. There were three thousand diaries for me to study. It was a long time ago. I remember now only one particular diary, in which a boy faithfully recorded that for four half-hours he had been 'firing stones, firing stones, firing stones … firing stones'.

What dilemmas he must have been wrestling with! What solutions he must have entertained! What meandering he must have done!

Astrud Gilberto Saves Ireland!

IN 1994, THE GREAT SCHOLAR FRANK Mitchell published a monograph entitled *Where Has Ireland Come From?* It was a slim volume, but in its sixty pages Frank took us on a magic carpet journey of seventeen hundred million years, outlining how this lump of rock we live on came to be where it is and in the shape that it is. I was intrigued and asked Frank if he would make that journey in a radio series. He agreed and I arrived at his room in Trinity College with microphone and tape recorder on a bright June afternoon – to 'make a start'.

The start takes us back down those seventeen hundred million years to when 'Ireland' was located in southern latitudes at about the level of South Africa … A fascinating beginning. Four hours later I stagger out into the Dublin sunshine with the entire series on tape – a four-hour journey which would be edited into thirteen quarter-hour programmes. I am – almost literally – left speechless by the energy and enthusiasm of this amazing man, now in his ninth decade. He insisted on keeping going once he had built up a head of steam, and was as fresh as ever when he concluded his fantastic journey with a look at Irish farming at the end of the twentieth century. He declines the offer of a meal as he is anxious to get to his home in the Boyne Valley, before setting out tomorrow for an archaeological dig in Valentia, Co. Kerry.

And what, I hear you ask, has Astrud Gilberto to do with all of this? Simple. I ran out of tape and to conclude the interview I had to record over a tape of Astrud's hits which I had in my bag. Sorry Astrud, but thanks.

The Return

I SPENT FIVE YEARS OF MY LIFE IN THE 1950S as a boarder in the then Patrician College, Ballyfin, Co. Laois. As a school it is no more. The house and estate – originally the home of the Coote family – were sold to an American magnate, Fred Krehbiel, in 2002. He had a dream of restoring them to their original grandeur and that dream was realised when Ballyfin Hotel opened its doors on 1 May 2011. It is expensive but I felt that, having experienced the spare and spartan Ballyfin of the fifties, I just had to sample the luxury and opulence of twenty-first century Ballyfin. And so I presented myself at the mansion doors on Sunday, 1 May.

The transformation was awesome. As students we had little to do with the mansion itself – the school was a separate block – but one room we knew well was the oratory. This was now restored to its original function – the State Dining Room. As we dined on West Cork scallops and pan-roasted fillet of beef, I reflected on our Sunday treat as boarders – a spoonful of jam to go with the tea, bread and butter. We ate that in the refectory, where before dinner I now had a relaxing swim. It is now a state-of-the-art swimming pool. I booked myself in for a massage next day in the treatment room – the vegetable store of our schooldays.

On my first night as a frightened twelve year old, I shared a dormitory with fifty other boys. Tonight I have an entire sumptuous suite to myself, overlooking the mesmerising cascade that has been built into the sloping grounds outside. Nothing has been spared in restoring this beautiful house to its former grandeur. I thought of the sacrifice my parents had made for me nearly sixty years ago. And after dinner when I entered the gents' toilet and realised I was in the former office of the college President, I didn't know whether to laugh or cry …

Eccentrics

THEY ARE BY DEFINITION 'OFF-CENTRE' – persons 'whose behaviour is habitually unusual or whimsical' (OED). We have all met them. Often they become figures of fun. The writer John McGahern met them in the persons of Mr Moroney and his son, neighbours of the young John who had 'a farm they never looked after'. It was in the Moroneys' house that John discovered books, coming himself from 'a house that had no books'. In a radio interview, he told me how he was sent to Moroneys to buy a bag of apples for half a crown, and fell into conversation with the old man about books.

'When I was about eleven, he gave me the run of his excellent nineteenth-century library. For about eight or nine years, I would come every fortnight, returning five or six books and taking away five or six more in my oil-cloth shopping bag.' He read everything they had to offer. 'I don't think I differentiated between Zane Grey and Dickens. I just read for pleasure.'

The Moroneys were truly eccentric. They lived on tea, bread and jam and would only wash the delph when they had to – about once a month. Willie (the father) was a great beekeeper and had an enormous beard.

'When he was talking about books the jam on his bread fell into his beard, setting off a buzzing noise. Without interrupting the conversation, he extracted three or four bees from his beard, cast them off and carried on …' The son was interested in astronomy and once took John to spend a night on Sugarloaf Mountain studying the stars.

Eccentrics. Off-centre 'odd-bods'. But what a debt we owe them for introducing one of our great modern writers to the world of books.

The Music Box

I TRIPPED OVER MY OLD RECORD PLAYER IN the study the other day. It's redundant now of course, but once it was my pride and joy and I am loathe to consign it to the skip.

Fifty years ago, on graduation as a primary teacher, I wandered into the wonderland that was Pim's department store in South Great George's Street, Dublin. I was about to make my first major purchase as a wage-earner, although on a salary of five pounds ten shillings a week, my horizons were limited. I longed for a record player and when my eye fell on the sleek lines of the Bush Model 210 with a state-of-the-art Garrard turntable, it was love at first sight. Problem – it would cost me nearly a month's salary. The only option was hire-purchase. One guinea deposit and twenty monthly payments of a guinea.

A guarantor would be needed. I presented the form to my father. 'You will do no such thing,' he pronounced. The whole idea of hire-purchase would be anathema to his generation. You only bought something when you could pay for it. I was disconsolate, but then he did a wonderful thing. He went down to Pim's, bought the player for cash (which would have been difficult enough for him) and presented it to me. 'Now,' he said, 'you pay me a pound down and a pound a month until you pay it off.'

What pleasure that machine brought me over the years as I accumulated a collection of LPs and EPs. I made practical use of it in the classroom also, but my warmest memory is of my courting days. Sunday afternoons in a Whitehall flat, sharing a Tchaikovsky symphony with the love of my life.

The coming of the CD eventually spelt the end of the Bush 210, but it still retains a place in my heart – and in my study.

Nightlight

I DON'T MIND GROWING OLDER, BUT I HAVE a fear – as I suspect many people do – of growing enfeebled, confused and dependent on others. For years, when I worked in Dublin, I would pass a nursing home at night. I would think of the residents as they settled for the night when the nightlights were switched on – and I would wonder at what thoughts and imaginings they entertained …

NIGHTLIGHT

Approaching midnight
I pass by and look up.
Your nightlight barely lit.
As you lie there
I wonder
What spirits attend you
What ghosts shimmer
What moth-fears flit
In the spare light?

What voices call you
– father, mother, spouse
What voices you call –
Daughter, son, grandchild
And do they answer?

Enthusiasm

THERE IS A WONDERFUL STORY TOLD ABOUT the great cellist Jacqueline Du Pré. When she was a little girl of five or six, she turned up at music school for her first examination. She came bouncing along a corridor with an instrument as big as herself. A security man obligingly held the door open for her.

'Well,' he observed, 'you must have done very well in your test.'

'Oh no,' Jacqueline replied, 'I'm only going in to play *now!*'

The adult interpreted happiness as success, but the child was simply displaying enthusiasm. And enthusiasm means, 'to be inspired or possessed by a god'.

We need to be very careful not to stifle enthusiasm in the child.

Bears and Circuses

THERE ARE IMAGES THAT SEAR THEMSELVES into our memories of childhood, never to be erased. When I interviewed Tommy O'Brien, music collector and opera buff, on his childhood, he recalled some very vivid images.

'My earliest memory is of being about four, dressed in a pinafore, being taken by my brother on a dark winter's evening along the Dungarvan Road. There ahead of us was a swarthy-looking man leading a huge black bear on a chain – one of numerous street performers who came to our town then and put on a show, hoping to earn a few pence. They were on their way to the next town, Ardfinnan.

'And then there were the circuses – Duffys, Buffalo Bill's, Hannafords.' The arrival of the circus in the town of Clonmel was a spectacular event. There were no motorised cavalcades – it was all horse-drawn wagons. The entry of the circus, usually at about eleven o'clock on a Monday morning, was billed by Duffys as 'The Grand Procession – a mile of glittering splendour'. It might not have been a mile, but it stretched right through the town – wagons, camels, elephants, cages of lions, acrobats performing on the street as they went, cowboys on horseback doing stunts with lassoes as they passed. It was one great free show – nearly as good as the circus performance itself.

'I think we paid twopence to sit on a hard seat but it was always a great show. One year the top of the bill attraction was Willie Kantor and his Midgets. They were wonderful acrobats and high-wire performers. Years later, when I was in London for the opera season, I saw Willie and his troupe near the top of the bill in the Palladium, so they were world-class performers, and I had seen them in Duffys Circus in Clonmel.'

STOP PRESS!

2 MARCH 2011. WE JUST BEAT ENGLAND AT cricket in the World Cup. I think I should deconstruct that sentence. We – Ireland, a little island, home of five million people. Just beat England – cricket super-power, founding home of the game. At cricket – minority sport in Ireland; England recently won the Ashes in Australia. In the World Cup – not a 'friendly' on a damp wicket on a drizzly August evening in Rathmines, but in a sun-baked stadium in distant Bangalore in the white heat of the World Cup.

The headline writers have had a field day (pardon the pun) – *Bang go leor! How's THAT?* and *Johnston, Mooney and O'Brien Make Toast of England!* (brilliant!). And they did it the hard way, coming from 111 for 5 needing 328 to win. In soccer terms, being 6–0 down at half-time and winning 7–6. Kevin O'Brien hit the fastest century in World Cup history. The stuff of dreams. Reminds me of those heady days when I flayed the English bowling with my hurley, spraying sixes and fours all over our garden and that of Mrs Reynolds next door. (May I modestly add that in the same week I scored the winning goal for Meath in the All-Ireland final and beat Lew Hoad in the Wimbledon Men's Singles final – who will forget that UNBELIEVABLE winning backhand?)

Our Taoiseach-elect, Enda Kenny, in congratulating the cricketers said, 'With self-belief, the seemingly impossible can become possible.' We all hope their victory will lift our spirits from the mire of recession, just as Jack's Army gave us hope at Italia '90 as we emerged from the dark eighties. But for now, savour the words – *We just beat England at cricket in the World Cup.* And remember the date – 2 March 2011.

Drains and Radiators

I MET MY FRIENDS AND MENTORS CHARLES and Elizabeth Handy again today. They are giving a three-day seminar in Kelly's Hotel, Rosslare, on the theme 'Re-thinking Your Life'. Good positive stuff for the times we live in. I joined them for lunch afterwards and somehow the subject of friends came up.

'We divide our friends into drains and radiators,' Elizabeth announced. My curiosity was aroused. 'Do explain, please.' 'Well, it's obvious, isn't it?' she replied. 'The drains tend to moan and whinge and complain about *everything* – the government, the weather, the cost of living, the local cricket team. They simply drain the energy out of you. An hour in their company and you are flat!' 'And the older they get, the worse they get,' Charles added.

And the radiators? 'Well, they're such fun to be with! They are warm and positive and cheering and we are so at ease in their company.' 'They radiate energy?' I suggested.

'Exactly.' Elizabeth replied with a 'thank-you-for-stating-the-obvious' look. A horrible thought crossed my mind – I hope I am not one of their drains … 'So what can you do?' I countered quickly. 'We try and see the drains as seldom as possible,' Charles said in his wonderful matter-of-fact tone.

There is a moral here. I am currently re-appraising my list of friends.

Regarding Clichés

OH JOY! A HAPPY CONFLUENCE OF TWO other moments – 'Bookmarks' and 'A Sixpenny Treasure'. Today in leafing through that sixpenny treasure, I found secreted among its pages a cutting from the Letters Page of the *Irish Times*, 8 January 1965 – my first published letter! It was written in response to a leader about clichés …

Dear Sir,

At last, like a bolt from the blue, the cliché has been dealt a shattering blow through the medium of your influential paper. In these modern times it seems to be a *sine qua non* of most political speeches and, *inter alia*, public outcries that they should be riddled with clichés. Indeed, it is a well-nigh indisputable fact that the State of Clichéria is governed by a tyrannical triumvirate, *Pro Bono Publico, Fiat Iustitia* and *Vox Populi.*

Sportswriters have reached prodigious heights, economists have never had it so good and, while film critics may have been run of the mill, all have done Trojan work in the service of the state of chassis, sorry Clichéria.

Too long have we been content to let sleeping dogs lie and play second fiddle. Now that the wind of change blows through the proper channels – *mirabile visu!* – there must be no more beating about the bush. With chins up and putting our best feet forward, let us prepare for the Titanic struggle ahead. The torch has been passed on. Down with Clichéria – *en bloc!*

Yours etc.

Well maybe I was young and naive, but I still subscribe to those views, by and large …

Two Hundred Valentines

AS A WRITER OF CHILDREN'S FICTION, I AM honoured to be invited to schools to talk about writing. Today – Valentine's Day 2011 – I paid my fourth visit to a quite extraordinary school – St Mark's Primary School, Springfield, Tallaght. I love visiting this school – it radiates warmth and welcome, generated by a dynamic principal and an enthusiastic staff. But of course it is the children that win you over in their eagerness to know the world, their natural enthusiasm and above all in their diversity. St Mark's has forty-seven different nationalities on its roll – children whose parents have come from Africa, India, Eastern Europe, the Baltic States and more besides. The school is like a mini United Nations and its diverse population is totally at ease.

Today I met six fifth classes over two sessions. They have never met a 'writer' before. I tell them that I didn't ever meet one either when I was a child (about two thousand years ago …) – all the writers were dead. But hey, look! I'm alive, an ordinary human (only one head!) but possessing four special attributes. I'm a *sponge* (open, attentive, observant), a *magpie* (a collector of ideas, stories, words), a *daydreamer* (full of imagination – daydreaming is good!) and a *cat* (full of curiosity, which will never kill me!).

The children are so lively and eager, full of questions (Where do you get ideas? How long does it take to write a book? What was your favourite book as a child?) – a joy to be with. I fear for what the 'system' will ultimately do to them – to Ryan, Jamie, Natasha, Camille, Lucan, Chinamelu … But for now they are happy to be learning and to be together in this wonderful school.

Rite of Passage

I STIRRED MYSELF SLUGGISHLY, TRYING TO come up with excuses to avoid the moment. The usual suspects – a twinge in the back, maybe tomorrow would be a better day, maybe it's too soon to attempt this operation – but I couldn't convince myself. My accomplice seemed equally unenthusiastic – quite content to rest easy on this Sunday afternoon as he had done for many Sundays now. 'Come on,' I said. 'I'm giving up a match on telly for this, so you can make the effort also.'

After a little persuasion, he relented. We made a start. Progress was slow initially. It is a boringly repetitive operation but we eventually got into a rhythm to the point where it was almost pleasurable. My accomplice droned on but gradually I became atttuned to his monotone. Another of his type seemed to be answering him from further down the road.

The sunshine was warm. There was a pleasant westerly breeze. Maybe it wasn't as difficult as I had feared. And then came that reassuring scent. Freshly cut grass drying in the April sunshine. I savoured it as I completed the last few laps. A pat of commendation to my accomplice as I returned him to his shed. After all it had only taken three tugs on the starting cord to get him going after the long winter. And with luck I will catch the end of the match.

First cut of the season. Life is good. *Summer is icumen in.*

Butterflies

STARTLED BY A BUTTERFLY? HOW COULD YOU be startled by a butterfly? Well, when it appears out of season, in the middle of winter, fluttering against a window pane in all its fragile beauty. I remember one extraordinary butterfly 'resurrection' incident – fittingly at the Easter Vigil Mass in Greystones, many years ago. The butterfly kept hovering over the altar, occasionally disappearing before swooping down over the priest's head. Then at the exact moment of the Consecration it alighted on the chalice. What a thrilling resurrection image!

Fast forward to Christmas Day 2001 – the dreaded first Christmas after my wife's death in June of that year. In fact, she died on 25 June, so this would be her six-month anniversary. A difficult, difficult day, but our family had come to our Galway home to be together for the first Christmas without Olive – a family that now included our first grandchild, Eva, born in August of that year.

We are seated at the Christmas dinner table, with a place set for the absent one. A sudden fluttering noise distracts me – a butterfly beating frantically against the window pane. It finds energy to lift away from the window, floats across the room, hovers and then lands thrillingly on the centre of the table. Fragile, beautiful, radiant, at rest.

The experts will tell you that a sudden sharp rise in temperature (Christmas Day cooking) will – temporarily – awaken the butterfly from his winter slumber, but I have my own views on this Christmas Day. Here to join us is the spirit of someone who was fragile, beautiful and radiant and who is never more than a flutter of wings away.

In Coole Park

I STAND BENEATH ONE OF IRELAND'S MOST famous and most beautiful trees, the magnificent copper beech in Coole Park, Co. Galway. It's known as the Autograph Tree. Here in Coole Park, Lady Augusta Gregory played hostess to some of the greatest names in the literary and artistic world at the turn of the twentieth century. She asked her visitors to leave their autographs by carving their initials on the bark of the copper beech. An ecologically incorrect invitation by twenty-first-century standards, but her guests complied and a century later their initials are still decipherable:

G(eorge)B(ernard)S(haw),
J(ohn)M(asefield)
A(ugustus)J(ohn)
D(ouglas)H(yde)
W(illiam)B(utler)Y(eats)
S(eán)O'C(asey)
J(ohn) M(illington)S(ynge)

V(iolet)M(artin)
J(ack)B(utler)Y(eats)

The list goes on.

But while I am in awe of that list, I am if anything even more in awe of this beautiful, beautiful tree. Standing in its shelter on this damp summer evening, I am overwhelmed by its majesty. Its great height dwarfs me to insignificance. Its graceful boughs sweep down symmetrically to brush the lush grass beneath. At this time of year, clothed in its copper mantle, it is breathtaking to gaze upon. It is the perfect tree.

An Ordinary Ould Sunday

A TYPICAL OULD MONDAY! THAT EXPRESSION stays with me from a James Plunkett story. A man jumps onto the platform of a city bus (we are talking 1960s here), surveys the dull damp world about him and sighs to the conductor – 'Ah, a typical ould Monday!'

But is any ould Monday 'typical'? Or Tuesday? Or *any* day? Every day has its bits and pieces, some of which we can cherish. I reflected on this shortly after my wife died, when I wrote these lines …

I went for a walk
On an ordinary ould Sunday
Children in buggies
Dogs being walked
Old people helped along
Garrulous families
Young lovers hand in hand
A tidy-up of the garden
A clean-out of the car

And I thought

How many ordinary ould Sundays
Did we spend
Cooking the lunch
Taking the children out
Walking the dog
Tidying the garden
Lazing?

By my reckoning
About sixteen hundred …
Sixteen hundred
Ordinary ould Sundays
And now
Not a one in sight.

Right Pleasure

I AM STANDING IN GEORGE CUNNINGHAM'S Lawnmower Shed … surrounded by books! George is a contemporary of mine and he has been a life-long collector of books. The collection began in his converted garage which begat Extension One, which begat Extension Two, which begat the 'Lawnmower Shed'. The lawnmower is still homeless, but the book collection is a bibliophile's joy and continues to grow.

Today George places in my hand the oldest book in his collection – an incomplete copy of *On Right Pleasure and Good Health*, written in Italian by Bartholomew Sacchi, known as Platina, and published in Venice in 1494. Platina was a mercenary soldier, a tutor and ultimately the Vatican librarian under Pope Sixtus IV. His book is often referrred to as the first cookery book and indeed there are chapters on food, from the ordinary to the exotic. But there are other areas of interest, e.g. 'to ensure pleasure in life'. Here we are advised that from 6 February to 8 May 'the blood increases' and it is the safest time to have sex, while from 8 May to 6 August 'choler rises' and sex should be totally avoided.

What really excites me, of course, is that I hold in my hand pages printed over five hundred years ago, when printing was in its infancy … A book that was printed when news was filtering through that Columbus had discovered a New World, printed ten years before Leonardo painted the Mona Lisa … It is far beyond 'right pleasure' to touch these delicate pages which had been fashioned by a Venezian printer half a millennium ago. What other hands had held and perused them, I can only muse, here in a lawnmower shed in a Tipperary town.

Anniversary Gift

25 JUNE 2011. IT IS THE TENTH ANNIVERSARY of the death of my wife Olive. As always, I have returned to Rosslare, Co. Wexford, the place where she died. Our son Declan joins me for the anniversary Mass and later for dinner. Over dinner, he shows me two 'photographs'. They are scans of the first baby he and Kelly are expecting in December. What an anniversary gift!

Welcome, little one!

I wish you a safe arrival into the world. May you always experience love and being cherished.

The world you will grow into will be unrecognisable from the world I entered seventy years ago. Then there was war. Now we have peace. Then and now, sadly, there is uncertainty and doubt – but there is also that immense ocean of possibility stretching before you. May you never shirk exploring that ocean, armed with the unfailing gift of imagination.

Little unborn one, safe in the warmth of your mother's womb, may you have a long and healthy life. May you always be curious, for that way learning lies.

May you have a lifelong love of words and know their possibility too.

May you always be surrounded by music that will transport you to wild horizons.

May you be familiar with quiet too and readily engage silence as your friend.

May you always know that however heavily life may buffet you, you are loved and cherished by your family and by previous generations you will never know. May you be happy in that knowledge and never without hope.

Little one, you have so much to live for. We all await your joining us to begin that great adventure.

Welcome!

Making Contact

I HAVE LOVED BRIAN FRIEL'S *Philadelphia, Here I Come* since I first saw it in Dublin nearly fifty years ago. Apart from enjoying it as a drama, I have used it as a teacher and as a radio producer to illustrate the importance of communication within a family.

Gar O'Donnell is about to emigrate to Philadelphia, and as he sits down for his final meal with his father S.B. (whom he addresses privately as 'Screwballs') he craves one unpredictable remark from him, something other than a reference to the number of rats that have been around his store. This is the heartbreaking moment when Private Gar (the 'man within') directs his interior thoughts at his father.

Screwballs … we embarrass one another. If one of us were to say 'You're looking tired' or 'That's a bad cough you have', the other would fall over backways with embarrassment. So tonight, do you know what I want you to do? I want you to make one unpredictable remark, and even though I'll still be on that plane tomorrow morning, I'll have doubts: maybe I should have stuck it out; maybe the old codger did have feelings; maybe I have maligned the old bastard. So now, Screwballs, say … 'Once upon a time a rainbow ended in our garden' … Say 'I like to walk across the White Strand when there's a misty rain falling' … Say 'Gar, son.' Say 'Gar, you bugger you, why don't you stick it out here with me, for it's not such a bad oul bugger of a place'. Go on! Say it! Say it! Say it!

S.B.: True enough.

PUBLIC GAR: Aye?

S.B.: I didn't find as many about the year.

Beautiful People

I HAVE LONG BEEN AN ADMIRER OF JEAN Vanier, the founder of the *L'Arche* movement, which enables people with learning disability to live in community. I had the privilege of interviewing him when he came to County Galway some years ago …

'I think *L'Arche* is a discovery that people with handicaps are beautiful people. They may be slow and more fragile, but if they are loved and appreciated, they are incredibly beautiful. They have great wisdom, but most of the time they are pushed aside. People don't listen to them, so they are unable to give out their beauty, their wisdom and their kindness …'

On a beautiful July afternoon some years later I was honoured to welcome a *L'Arche* group from Belfast to my home. They were on their way with their director, Maria Garvey, to their annual holiday in Ballyvaughan, Co. Clare. I had invited them to stop off for a picnic. Just to be in the company of these beautiful young people seemed to make the sun shine even more brightly. Gillian, who reminded us continually in song – 'I am beautiful'. Geoffrey, who insisted on holding my hand as we strolled around the garden. Thomas, the severely damaged one, the silent one. What wondering engaged him? And Larry, beautiful Larry, the mystic who spends literally hours each day watching the clouds.

A beautiful afternoon with beautiful people. As they waved goodbye I could hear Jean Vanier's words echoing around my garden.

The Wisdom of Three Poets

WHILE PREPARING A TALK ON THE THEME 'Reflections on Ageing', I came across some powerful words by the Mexican writer, Octavio Paz ….

> With great difficulty, advancing by millimetres each year, I carve a road out of the rock. For millennia, my teeth have wasted and my nails broken to get there, to the other side, to the light and the open air … I have spent the second part of my life breaking the stones, drilling the walls, smashing the doors, removing the obstacles I placed between the light and myself in the first part of my life.

For me there is much wisdom and truth in those words, but rather than seem an occasion for darkness and regret, they are more a great call to freedom and possibility. As Paz indicates, we carry many self-made burdens into later life. Old age need not be a burdensome time. It is a time when, as John O'Donohue advises, we should 'feast on our lives'. A time of harvest, when we should reap and sift the rewards of experience. A time when, as John inimitably put it, we should 'be "careless", show a bit of ould wildness'.

Or as Seamus Heaney put it in 'Station Island':

> *Let go, let fly, forget*
> *You've listened long enough.*
> *Now strike your note.*

Daydreaming

HOW MANY OF US REMEMBER BEING reprimanded as children with the words, 'Are you daydreaming again? Do you ever listen to me? You're always dreaming!' Worse still, how many of us have reprimanded our own children or students with those same words? Far from being a BAD THING, daydreaming is a good and necessary exercise. (Terms and conditions apply, of course.) Tony Buzan, who writes and lectures extensively on memory and learning, puts it quite bluntly:

'Daydreaming is a great gymnasium for the mind where the imagination exercises and plays. You have to daydream. If you don't, you die.'

Writers, artists, scientists, inventors spend a lot of time in that gymnasium, wondering, weaving.

When I visit schools as a writer, I set children a little exercise. 'Close your eyes for ten seconds. Be very still. Now go wherever you want to go – anywhere in the whole wide world.' And so they become intrepid jungle explorers, heroic performers in the Nou-Camp or Croke Park, shoppers in Paris or New York, visitors to Candyland, lazy sunseekers in Lanzarote or crazy Formula One drivers. But not all of them. I recall the girl who just wanted to be in her granny's kitchen or the boy who was 'drawing home bales with Tommy Brennan's tractor'. I love that.

A Chance Remark

OUT IN EAST CONNEMARA AS YOU TRAVEL through Joyce country from Maam Cross to Clonbur, there is a magnificent lake called Loughnafooey. I am told it means 'the lake of the winnowing winds'. It has a special place in my heart, for it was there, on an August afternoon in 1967, that I proposed to the love of my life, Olive. Amazingly and thankfully, she said yes. Maybe she was intoxicated with the beauty of the place … It was a beautiful day. It was a beautiful place. And her beauty outshone both. We never went back there together, but since she died I have gone back several times to recapture the memory.

Fast forward nearly forty years. It is 2005. I am in Argentina with a group from Galway. It is Palm Sunday. We embark on a two-hundred-kilometre coach journey westward from Mendoza into the foothills of the Andes. The route followed that of the amazing Trans-Andean Railway, built in the nineteenth century. The scenery grew more spectacular as we neared the Chilean border. In the distance lay the majestic snow-capped Aconcagua Mountain – yet we were assailed by a warm wind known as the Zonda. It was an exhilarating experience.

On the return journey, one of our group, a Connemara woman, made a chance remark. She knew nothing of my story, but as she looked out she mused aloud – 'Wouldn't parts of this place remind you of Loughnafooey?' I felt warm all over. It had nothing to do with the Zonda.

Me and Daniel - A Weather Conversation

ME: What a day! That wind would skin you. Typical north-easterly.

DANIEL: Winds! All bless the Lord, give glory and eternal praise to him.

ME: The days are drawing in. I dread the thought of winter.

DANIEL: Nights and days! Bless the Lord, give glory and eternal praise to him.

ME: Don't you just hate November? All that fog and rain would depress you.

DANIEL: Dews and sleets! Bless the Lord, give glory and eternal praise to him.

ME: You can have your snow! A novelty at first but then it freezes and then more of it. No thanks!

DANIEL: Ice and snow! Bless the Lord, give glory and eternal praise to him.

ME: And then come the floods! Rivers bursting their banks. Homes destroyed.

DANIEL: Seas and rivers! Bless the Lord, give glory and eternal praise to him.

ME: Must be the worst winter for years. Will it ever end?

DANIEL: Frost and cold! Bless the Lord, give glory and eternal praise to him.

ME: But –

DANIEL: All things the Lord has made, bless the Lord, give glory and eternal praise to him.

Adapted from the Book of Daniel (Old Testament)

A Quare Quiz

AS PRODUCER OF THE OPEN MIND programme, I instituted the Open Mind New Year's Family Quiz, which ran annually for ten years. It was deliberately difficult and long – the length was dictated by the year in question, e.g. in 1995 there were ninety-five questions. I usually allowed two weeks for its completion. Listeners loved the challenge of it – one man told me he rang Covent Garden in London about a question on ballet – and librarians ran for cover! The rise of the internet made it more difficult to set questions but it was fun while it lasted!

A typical question might be: 'An historic location, a teacher and a jazz singer combine for a lively dance.' The answer was (of course) Tarantella (TARA + N.T. + ELLA) ...

My favourite question of all was: 'Why are you afraid of this Grand National winner?'

The reference was to Vincent O'Brien's horse 'Quare Times', which won the Grand National in 1956. At least we Irish knew him as Quare Times (rhyming with Rare Dimes) but the classically trained BBC Radio announcer proclaimed the winner as 'Qua-re Tim-es' (Latin – Why are you afraid?).

I still have a vision of the locals in a bookie's shop somewhere in Tipperary saying, 'Jaykers, O'Brien's horse wasn't even in the first three ...'

In the Presence of Holiness

EIGHT-FIFTEEN A.M. IS AN UNUSUAL TIME to be entering a sports arena, but that is what I am doing this April morning – and I am not alone. Hundreds are filing into the University of Limerick Sports Arena with me, and by nine o'clock over three thousand people are seated in this huge facility. There is an expectant buzz in the air. We have not come to witness a sports event, however. For the next hour we are treated to music, song, chant and dance from Christian, Muslim and Jewish traditions, but this is only a prelude to the main event.

At 10.40 a.m., to rapturous applause, His Holiness the fourteenth Dalai Lama of Tibet is introduced to the waiting throng. Dressed in his colourful Buddhist robes and slightly stooped, there is something warm and enriching in his smiling demeanour. He has come to speak on 'The Power of Forgiveness' but his theme is Compassion. His message is simple. We are all the same at the basic primary level. At a secondary level we differ in our beliefs and there is too much emphasis on this level. A rapt audience clings to this serene man's every word. We are in the presence of holiness but there is great happiness emanating from this man. He engages us with little jokes and we warm to his chuckle. Who does that chuckle remind me of? Of course – Homer Simpson!

We all strive for inner peace, but too self-centred an attitude closes our 'inner door'. We all have the same potential for compassion but we need to develop that innate seed of compassion to extend our concern beyond our friends and ultimately to our enemies. Inner peace comes at a mental, not a material level. A simple message from a humble man. And I loved his Homer Simpson chuckle.

The Miracle of Us

IN HIS WORK AS A HERBALIST, SEÁN BOYLAN regards a book entitled *Fearfully and Wonderfully Made* as his bible. It is the story of an orthopaedic surgeon, Paul Brand, and the miracle that is the human body – a miracle we take so much for granted. Brand quotes St Augustine in this regard:

> Men go abroad to wonder at the height of mountains, at the huge waves of the sea, at the long courses of the rivers, at the vast compass of the ocean, at the circular motion of the stars; and they pass by themselves without wondering …

Here is Brand on the miracle of the human foot:

> Twenty-six bones line up in each foot – about the same number as in each hand. Even when a soccer player subjects these small bones to a cumulative force of over one thousand tons per foot over the course of a match, his living bones endure the violent stress, maintaining their elasticity. Not all of us leap and kick, but we do walk some sixty-five thousand miles – or more than two and a half times around the world – in a lifetime. Our body weight is evenly spread out through architecturally perfect arches which serve as springs, and the bending of knees and ankles absorbs stress.

Walking miracles, each and every one of us!

Brendan

AS A WRITER FOR CHILDREN, I LOVE TO GET letters from my readers. One such letter arrived some years ago from Brendan in County Longford. Unusually, it was typed. Brendan wanted to know when my next publication was due. 'I have enjoyed your three novels. My home tuition teacher read them to me and I thought they were very visual … Even though I have Spina Bifida and am blind, I love books and yours are the greatest. I would love to meet you some time …' Even though his teacher had typed the letter he still managed to inscribe his initials over the 'signature'.

Of course I must visit him, I thought. The poor lad, doubly handicapped – what a confined and depressing life he must lead. And I did visit him. How wrong could I be! One of the happiest children I have known, with a great big smile, full of chatter and 'divilment'. He loved to boss his big sisters into wheeling him down the town to meet people and exchange banter and gossip. How utterly wrong and presumptuous I was. I came away both chastened and energised. And I thought to myself – if no one but Brendan had ever bought my books, was not his enjoyment of them alone worth my writing them?

And so, when I visit schools, and children ask me lots of questions, including inevitably, 'Do you write books to make loads of money?' I read Brendan's letter to them.

That, I tell them, is why I write.

Up the Bridge!

And when the final whistle blew
We gave a mighty roar
The Bridge had truly skinned 'the Cats'
To the tune of double scores!

This particular moment came at 3.20 on the afternoon of St Patrick's Day, 2011. The place was Croke Park and referee Johnny Ryan's final whistle signalled that Clarinbridge had beaten O'Loughlin Gaels of Kilkenny in the All-Ireland Club Hurling Championship Final. Clarinbridge – All-Ireland Champions for the first time. For the team, for their supporters, for the whole 'Bridge community, a moment to savour and to continue savouring. Busloads of supporters had made the journey to Dublin, and when the team returned in triumph that night, it seemed that the entire parish, from babes-in-arms to pensioners, had thronged the village to féte their heroes.

And they *are* heroes, homebred heroes, local lads, neighbours' children, who had given their all 'for the credit of the little village', as Matt the Thrasher had done for Knocknagow in the hammer-throwing contest. There was and is a buzz in the air, a spring in all our steps, a pride in our place that only an achievement like this can bring. It was a victory for ancestors who founded the club 121 years ago, for old men who toiled on the field when nothing was won, and especially for the children who now have flesh and blood heroes to replace plastic popstars or pampered, overpaid footballers. Up the Bridge!

You gave us all a mighty lift
With that terrific show
Champions of All-Ireland
An Droichead Abú – go deo!

The Company of Books

A RECENTLY OPENED BOOKSHOP IN DUBLIN carries the name *The Company of Books*. What a well-chosen name! For books are assuredly the best of company. They cheer us, reassure us, inform us, relax us. Just the sight of them, jumbled there on a bookshelf, irregular in shape and size, dressed in a variety of jackets, is consolation enough to know we are not alone. 'Here we are,' they seem to say. 'Choose one of us and we will be your travelling companion, even though you need not leave your fireside chair. A well-thumbed Heaney volume, maybe? Thomas Pakenham's marvellous *Meetings with Remarkable Trees*? A much-savoured novel? Choose! Handle! Enjoy!'

To those who would dismiss such a notion, I offer the words of Jane Austen:

Oh, it's only a novel, only some work in which the greatest powers of the mind are displayed, in which the most thorough knowledge of human nature, the happiest delineation of its varieties, the liveliest diffusions of wit and humour are conveyed to the world in the best-chosen language.

The late Cardinal Cahal Daly, a lifelong bibliophile, once said to me that for him, just owning books and being in their presence is to some extent educative. There is a certain satisfaction in being surrounded by a wider world of ideas. And I recall making a documentary about the now defunct Greene's Bookshop. The owner, Eric Pembrey, bought a lifetime collection of books from an old lady who had to move into a nursing home. As he removed the books, she wept openly – not for the loss of her home or her independence, but for the loss of the company of her books.

The Beauty of Age

IT WAS THE HEADLINE IN THE *UCD NEWS* that attracted me –

Ninety-nine year old to lecture Folklore Dept.

I must meet and interview this man, I thought. And I did. He was Pádraig Mac Gréine, known in his homeplace of Ballinalee, Co. Longford, as 'Master Greene'. As a young teacher, he had collected material for the Irish Folklore Commission. It was a privilege to be in the company of such a gracious and wise man and to share the language and lore of a lost world that he had diligently recorded on index cards – Irish words in common use in his youth and Cant, the language of travellers. It was his enthusiasm for that lore and his curiosity about life that kept him forever young. He aged with serenity and contentment and lived to be 106. Having been born in 1900, his life touched three centuries.

Pádraig also aged with positivity (he renewed his driving licence for three years at the age of 102) and with activity (at 104, he was giving weekly lessons in Cant to young travellers). Quite simply, he taught those of us who were fortunate to know him how to live, how to age and how to die. This life, he would say, is but a preparation for the real life.

When he was a young man, Pádraig met a very old man whose aunt remembered meeting the starving French soldiers who landed in Killala in 1798. They were reduced to pulling rushes in the fields and eating the white pith of the roots. Living history in two backward leaps.

Writing Simple

HOW OFTEN HAVE YOU PUT DOWN A BOOK OR watched a film and said, 'I really enjoyed that. It was very simply done but it really held me'? Achieving that simplicity was no easy feat for the artist, however.

Jule Styne was one of the great popular songwriters of the twentieth century. Over a seven-decade career, he wrote some fifteen hundred songs, often in collaboration with lyricists such as Sammy Cahn. When he died in 1994, the London *Independent* devoted a large obituary notice to him. Underneath his photograph was a quote from the great man about his craft:

> Anyone can write clever. That's simple. But writing simple – that's real clever!

A very telling piece of wisdom, which I have tried to adopt as a motto in my own work, either in writing or in radio. For me, there is no greater compliment than to be told, 'That was a very simple story/programme …'

Making it simple was the real clever – and difficult – part.

Precious Stones

I TAKE A SMALL BOX DOWN FROM MY bookshelf. The name FROST BROS is embossed on the lid. Once it contained a piece of jewellery, but now it houses something more precious. The key is on the *side* of the box. Here I have written:

A stone and some mortar taken from the ruin of my mother's home, Derricknew, Killenaule, Co. Tipperary. 5.10.84

I never knew my Tipperary grandparents and to my regret I had never accompanied my mother to explore her Tipperary roots. She died in February 1984. Later that year I belatedly undertook that journey. It was quite an emotional trip. My guide, one of my mother's former neighbours, provided me with a pair of wellingtons as we had to traverse seven fields to reach the now derelict cottage where Patrick and Mary Ryan reared their eight children. The cottage stood alongside the Clonmel–Thurles railway line. Patrick had worked on the laying of that track. Decades later his son Jack helped lift the now defunct track.

I leaned against the wall of the cottage and tried to imagine how difficult life must have been for a girl born at the turn of the twentieth century. To school through the fields, indeed. Through seven gateways and seven fields before she even reached a roadway.

Instinctively, I broke off some mortar and dug a shard of stone out of the wall. A tenuous connection with my forebears, but a prized one. Frost Bros could never have supplied me with more precious stones.

Roger

I HAVE LONG ADMIRED THE POEMS OF ROGER
McGough. To many people he is simply the
master of the pun –

I have outlived
My youthfulness
So a quiet life for me.
Where once I used to
Scintillate
Now I sin
Till ten past three.

But his humour is always insightful
and his wit a torchlight in the dark.

Everyday
I think about dying,
About disease, starvation,
violence, terrorism, war,
the end of the world.

It helps
keep my mind off things.

I remember interviewing Roger in a bookshop
in Bray, Co. Wicklow. His mind is ever alert
to the possibilities of language. 'I was on my
way out here,' he told me, 'when I spied a
noticeboard outside a delicatessen. Printed
at the top was "TODAY'S SPECIAL".
They hadn't filled it in for today yet. I just
wanted to find some chalk and write
underneath – SO IS EVERYDAY!'

Out for the Day

ALL-IRELAND FINAL DAY – WHETHER IN football or hurling – is a unique day in Irish life. It is a very special day for the counties involved – a day of anticipation, passion, colour and ultimately for one county, celebration. It is the culmination of a long season of struggle and endeavour. Coming in September, it has all the elements of a harvest festival.

In 1988, I made a radio documentary entitled 'Final Day'. It attempted to capture the atmosphere of this unique day – the gathering of the fans, music and banter in the pubs, the sounds of the city, the thoughts of players and managers, the reactions of fans on the terraces. Above all, the enjoyment that this special day generates. In a way, the match itself was only secondary to the grand theatre it created (Meath and Cork played a draw!). For me, the magic of the day was encapsulated in the conversation of two Meath fans, caught on tape as they made their way out of Croke Park …

Sure, we're only out for the day!

Aye. This time next year we could be goin' down the road with a few flowers over us.

First Rose of Summer

SUDDENLY IT WAS THERE. After days of high winds and heavy squalls, it made its appearance, silently, without any pomp or parade. The annual miracle that is the rose. White, fragile and oh so fragrant, as I discovered when I bent to greet it with a kiss. It lifted my heart to see it dance in the breeze, unfolding its symmetry to the nourishing sun. This particular rose cheered me as it flowered on a bush I had planted some years ago in memory of another rose …

Today
Amid the cold, dark, drear
of November
I planted six roses.
My hands were winter-numb
As I kneaded
The raw earth
And yet I smiled
When I thought of
The summer memories
These frail roses
Would bring
Of you …
(NOVEMBER 2006)

I am reminded of the words of the seventeenth-century mystic, Angelus Silesius, when he described the rose as *ohne warum* – without why.

The rose is without why
She blooms because she blooms
She cares not for herself
Asks not if she is seen …

A Portrait of the Artist

IT IS DECEMBER 2007. I AM IN LANSDOWNE Road, but there is no rugby match in progress, for this is Lansdowne Road in West London and I am here to record an interview with Shirley Hughes, one of the great children's author-illustrators of our time. Now eighty years old, Shirley is as active and fecund with ideas as ever. Over afternoon tea she recalls her extraordinary career for me. In preparation for the interview, I have read her beautiful autobiography *A Life Drawing*, and to conclude the interview I ask Shirley to read from the closing chapter, as – for me – it gives a wonderful insight into the artistic process. She readily agrees.

'I get the juices flowing by squeezing out tubes of gouache colour onto a wet palette … You have to take a lot of risks, make lightning decisions, exploit the happy accident. It is, I imagine, rather like playing jazz. I do often play tapes of Benny Goodman, Art Tatum or Sidney Bechet. Their vitality drives me along.

'There is nothing so exciting, or so intimidating, as a blank piece of paper. You have to catch it unawares, sidle up nonchalantly and knock it for six with a good B pencil. A beautiful line is the thing … If things are going well and I have got hold of a brush which is just right and the washes are flowing sweetly, everything – from world concerns to family cares – goes quite out of my mind … However well you manage to realise your inner vision, at the end of the day you just have to hope you can take Ernest Hemingway's advice and leave it when you're going good. And, even though I know I haven't a hope of creating the images that were there in my head, attempting to do so is still the nearest thing I know to flying into the sun.'

Benedictus

WILL WE EVER HAVE A PROPER CONCERT hall in Galway? For years we have had to make do with Leisureland – a large auditorium which is part of the leisure complex – but its acoustics are poor and its sightlines, if you are on the level floor area, non-existent. Nevertheless, we welcome the occasional symphony concerts there. It's all we have.

Last night we welcomed the RTÉ Concert Orchestra and the Galway Baroque Singers – all ninety of them – for a performance of *The Armed Man: A Mass for Peace*, conducted by the composer Karl Jenkins. A very special performance of a compelling piece of work. An anguished cry against war –

The earth is full of anger. The seas are dark with wrath.

An impassioned cry for peace –

Ring out the narrowing lust of gold. Ring out the thousand wars of old.

The performers give their all, but even at ninety-strong, the singers are fighting the orchestra in the more powerful segments of the Mass. And then we come to the *Benedictus*. The exquisite strings offer a haunting and uplifting introduction to the voices and they respond with the most moving and enthralling prayer.

Benedictus

We are gently transported far beyond that great barn of an auditorium.

qui venit in nomine domini

We are the lark ascending, hovering above golden cornfields, borne ever higher by faith and hope and love. And there shall be no more death … Five minutes of utter beauty. *Benedictus*. We are singularly blessed.

Hosanna in excelsis.

At Rest

I AM ON A WRITER'S VISIT TO MULLAGH N.S., Co. Cavan. Shona comes up to me and proudly shows me the funeral Mass booklet for her great-uncle, T. P. McKenna. Of course, I remember – T. P. was buried here in his native place. I must visit his grave.

School visit over, I make my way to the old graveyard, behind the Church of Ireland church. The graveyard is in the form of a circular mound, atop which sits the ruin of a very old church – *Teampall Cheallaigh*. The graveyard itself dates back to the fourteenth century. The stones, time-worn and indecipherable, are markers of centuries of history. I love this place. The wind hushes through a giant beech tree. The countryside is drowning drowsily in whitethorn on this May afternoon. Across from me, Mullagh Lake shimmers in the sunshine. A pheasant krawks from a nearby meadow. Such a restful place.

I locate T. P.'s grave and congratulate him on his choice of resting-place. We have a chat about Cavan and Meath football. We agree that neither county will give us much cause for excitement this year. I look again at the verse in his funeral booklet.

In one of the stars I shall be living,
In one of them I shall be laughing
When you look at the sky at night ...
And when your sorrow is comforted,
You will be content that you have known me.
You will always be my friend,
You will want to laugh with me.

– ANTOINE DE SAINT EXUPÉRY

Excuse me, Ma'am

Excuse me, Ma'am
Was that you I just saw
Walking through the Garden of
    Remembrance
Alongside our President,
Past the shimmering pool
Reflecting a dull Dublin sky?
Did I see you slowly
Climb those steps
To face Oisin Kelly's sorrowful swans?

*We sent our vision aswim like a swan on the
river.*

Did I witness all this to the accompaniment
Of 'God Save the Queen'
Here in Parnell Square in Dublin?

*No man has the right to set a boundary
To the march of a nation.*

Did I see you accept a wreath
From an Irish army officer
And lay it

*To the memory of all those who gave
Their lives in the cause of Irish freedom?*

Excuse me Ma'am
Did I see you bow your head
And stand a silent minute
In the chill May morning air?

*O generations of freedom,
Remember us, the generations of the vision.*

Did I really witness all of this, Ma'am?
This moment of healing
This moment of hope

The vision became a reality.

Buíochas ó chroí, Ma'am.

17 May 2011

Garret

THERE WILL BE, DESERVEDLY, ACRES OF tributes written about our much-loved lost leader Garret FitzGerald – statesman, crusader, patriot – but the image that persists for many is a combination of the absent-minded professor wearing odd shoes and the kindly uncle who would make time to help a child build a Lego castle. For me, his kindness and courtesy shone like beacons at a time when such attributes were rare at a personal or political level.

I approached him for a 'tale out of school' to include in the book *Must Try Harder* – a fundraising venture for the Open Door Centre which my wife had co-founded. He was Taoiseach at the time, but found the time to send me this memory …

'When I was in my second year at school, I decided to show my appreciation of our Irish teacher, Tadhg Ó Murchú, whom I and the rest of the class felt to be both a good teacher and a very warm personality.

Since the age of seven or eight, I had been making toffee under the guidance of an elder brother, so I decided to make some toffee for Tadhg. Unfortunately, I nearly always under-cooked the toffee, which ended up in liquid form. I put it in a sweet tin and wrapped it very carefully with clear instructions to open it right side up. He received it with great pleasure, but when I came into class the next day I found that he was less pleased. He had failed to read my instructions (perhaps because they were written in English!) and had opened the tin the wrong side up, with the result that the contents had emptied themselves onto his carpet!'

Somehow, that is *so* Garret!

Strangers on a Train

21 MAY 2011. I DECIDE TO TRAVEL TO DUBLIN by train to pay my last respects to Garret. It's the least I can do. I am not alone. Two staunch Fine Gael men board the train at Tullamore.

There's two seats down the back. We'll be grand.
Sound job!

Isn't it strange too – Garret gone and Cosgrave still going strong?
Hard to credit …

God, they had to cut through some rock there, didn't they?
Aye and no big fancy machines in them days either.

You might sing it. There's Mickey Garry's field.

Good growth there. The bit of rain brought it on …

I suppose herself is back in London, walking the corgis.
Isn't she some woman for eighty-five?
Climbing all them steps.
And she's only five foot three.
Everything was so well done though.
Timed to the last second.
And beamed around the world. You'd be proud …

There's Tom Fennimore's cattle. Nice bit of beef.
And isn't that the plantation near your place?
Aye. They're clearing a sight of timber out of it …

There's Killenard. The golf-course. Did you ever play it?
Couldn't afford it! Now they're falling over themselves with special offers.

A lot of empty houses out there, aren't there?
Kildare's full of ghost estates.

I see DJ and the missus are in trouble too. Lost the run of themselves. What were they at, at all? …

Nice winter barley there. Doing well. Isn't it a great little plant to survive such a savage winter?

Bedad, we're nearly there! Never felt the journey.
What time is the last train back?

Quarter past six, I think. If all else fails, we can thumb it home.
Hah! That'd be some story!

Be Quiet!

IN 1991 WE MOVED HOUSE TO THE WEST coast of Ireland, to a two-storey thatched house at the end of a boreen leading to an inlet of Galway Bay. Negotiating that boreen was quite a task for the driver of the removals truck but he managed it – literally by inching his way along. He jumped out of the cab and surveyed the (to me) idyllic scene on a bright July morning. There was a long pause. 'Aye,' he sighed eventually. 'It's a grand place alright – if you could stand the quiet!' He was a true 'Dub' – a city man, who felt ill at ease at the lack of traffic noise, people chatter, all the normal bustle of city life. The occasional calling of a seabird or lowing of a cow were a poor substitute. There was too much 'quiet'.

His comment has stayed with me over the years. How uncomfortable we can be with stillness. Why do we fear silence, when – as John O'Donohue reminds us – it is 'the sister of the divine', helping us to unveil the riches of solitude? He quotes his great mentor Meister Eckhart who said that 'there is nothing in the world that resembles God so much as silence'. The French philosopher Pascal claimed that many of our major problems derive from our inability to sit still in a room. Modern life often insists that silence is a space that must be filled with clamour, music, noise. We need to embrace stillness more. Our own writer/philosopher John McGahern claimed that 'the best of life is lived quietly, where nothing happens but our calm journey through the day, where change is imperceptible and the precious life is everything.'

And Finally

I HAD, TO MY MIND, COMPLETED THIS anthology in May 2011 when my daughter Deirdre rang me from Montauk, Long Island.

'Do you want to hear a cool story?'

'Of course.'

'I was driving up Montauk Highway this morning when up ahead I saw the mangled corpse of a deer on the roadside. Another unfortunate casualty of the busy traffic on this highway. It happens all too regularly, despite warning signs to drive carefully. I averted my eyes from the bloody mess, when right in front of me I saw a small bundle on the roadway. I swerved to avoid it, pulled in on the hard shoulder and ran back.

'Incredibly, it was a newborn baby deer, covered in afterbirth and – amazingly – alive! I picked it up and took it back to my truck where I had some old towels. I cleaned it down and already it was mewling and squirming in my arms. I jumped into the truck, held the deer in my left arm and drove the twenty-minute journey to the veterinary surgery in Easthampton. The staff were amazed to find that the baby hadn't a mark on it. Obviously it had the protection of its mother's womb. They fed it and said they would pass it on to Animal Rescue. When I phoned my friend Pam later, she told me she had witnessed the impact and saw something spinning in the air. The poor deer's head, she thought. It was obviously the baby … Isn't that a cool story?'

More than cool. To think of new life emerging from carnage is just so uplifting. And I am so proud of my daughter for her part in the rescue.

Thank You for the Moments

Olive McKeever, Seamus Heaney, Ruby Murray, John O'Donohue, Hugh and Bridie Quinn, Ray Conniff, Sandra Reynolds, Gay Byrne, Seán Boylan, Uncle John, David Attenborough, John McGahern, Lisa, Deirdre and Declan Quinn, Roger McGough, Ben Zander, P. J. Ruane, Patrick Moore, George Green, Aunt Katie, T. P. McKenna, Michael Coady, Heels Dunne, Bryan McMahon, Anne and Catherine Gregory, Brian Leyden, Johnny Kelly, Seán Ó Faoláin, Spike Milligan, Uncle Jimmy, Mike Cooley, Ewan McColl and Peggy Seeger, Mickey and Gertie Sheridan, Peter Ustinov, Tommy O'Brien, Noel Quinn, Frank Mitchell, Dermot Morgan, Brian Friel, Patricia Heeney, Michael Monaghan, Karl Jenkins, Loughnafooey, George Mitchell, Paddy Graham, Francis Ledwidge, Ger Loughnane, Michael Kelly, Jule Styne, Tim Lehane, Robyn Rowland, Cloneycavan Man, Charles Handy, Dwight Eisenhower, Dorothy Edwards, Jean Vanier, Pádraig Mac Gréine, Jacqueline Du Pré, John D. Sheridan, Penelope Leach, Frank McNally, Terry McDonagh, Skellig Rock, Thomas Pakenham, Marie Louise O'Donnell, Lyndon Johnson, John Henry Newman, Seán McBride, Benny Goodman, Ballyfin, John A. Costello, Acker Bilk, Darragh Henehan, Shirley Hughes, the Irish Cricket Team, J. D. Meiklejohn, Cows, Brendan Hayes, Leo Tolstoy, Bhutan, Albert Einstein, Ballivor, Patricia Koppman, Gordon Wilson, Bill Kelly, Harry Garry, Colm Murtagh, Ted and Bobby Kennedy, Stan O'Brien, Fr Eamonn Dermody, the Friends of Sally Hardiman, Bobby, Lizzie Coyne, George Shearing, Lord Tennyson, Highgate Cemetery, BBC Television Natural History Unit, Astrud Gilberto, Platina, the Robin, Daniel, Butterflies, Octavio Paz, William Wordsworth, the Clarinbridge Hurling Team, the Dalai Lama, Queen Elizabeth II, the White Rose, Garret FitzGerald, Strangers on a Train, and so many children I have been privileged to meet. Oh, and did I mention Olive McKeever?

Epilogue

NOEL

The phone rings. I have expected this moment, but I don't want to experience it. Answer it! Yes, it is the news I feared. Noel is gone. Finally succumbed to a long battle with cancer. Noel. Big Brother by two years. ONLY BROTHER. PAL.

The memory-moments unfold. Bitterly fought hurling games in our childhood backyard, when invariably Mother would have to mediate, following yet another meleé in the turf-shed goal. To cool our passions, we were sent to draw endless buckets of water from the village pump, running a hurley through the bucket handle so that we could share the load. BROTHER. OPPONENT. PAL.

He dreamed one night of a pink horse under the stairs. I was totally convinced – and totally scared. For a long time I didn't dare look. BROTHER. DREAMER. PAL.

Boarding school. It was good to have a brother a year ahead of me. To look out for me. Stand up for me. Ease the way. BROTHER. BIG BROTHER. PAL.

Life. We take our different paths, but they cross at family rituals. Joys and sorrows shared. Triumphs and tragedies. BROTHER. SUPPORT. PAL.

And now the fever of life is over and your work is done. The final voyage. I pray that gentle winds will waft you to the promised shore on waves of love and gratitude. BROTHER. LOVED ONE. PAL.

At every moment
There is a moment
To be seized
So seize it
There and then!
For you know
That you will never have
That moment
Again.

John Quinn